DATE DUE

DEC 1 7 1996	
OCT 5 1999	
DEC 12 1999	

GAYLORD

SCHOOL DAYS, FUN DAYS

ABOUT THE AUTHOR

Deborah Hill is a doctor of romance languages and linguistics. Her grade school teaching experiences include working with retarded children in the Panama Canal Zone's Curundu Elementary School and teaching E.S.L. at Junipero Serra Elementary in Long Beach, California. She is currently a full-time writer and lecturer, specializing in humor studies and international education. She is also the author of *Humor in the Classroom: A Handbook for Teachers and Other Entertainers* (Charles C Thomas, 1988).

ABOUT THE ARTIST

David R. Caperton is a cartoonist, high school English and Drama teacher and stand-up comedian who draws on his experiences in the classroom for much of his humor. His comic strip, "Mr. C.," has appeared in *NEA Today*. He and his wife, Suzanna, live and teach in Columbus, Ohio.

SCHOOL DAYS, FUN DAYS

Creative Ways to Teach Humor Skills
in the Classroom

By

DEBORAH J. HILL, PH.D.

Illustrated by

David R. Caperton

CHARLES C THOMAS • PUBLISHER
Springfield • Illinois • U.S.A.

Published and Distributed Throughout the World by

CHARLES C THOMAS • PUBLISHER
2600 South First Street
Springfield, Illinois 62794-9265

© *1993 by* CHARLES C THOMAS • PUBLISHER
ISBN 0-398-05862-8
Library of Congress Catalog Card Number: 93-7241

With THOMAS BOOKS *careful attention is given to all details of manufacturing
and design. It is the Publisher's desire to present books that are satisfactory as to their
physical qualities and artistic possibilities and appropriate for their particular use.*
THOMAS BOOKS *will be true to those laws of quality that assure a good name
and good will.*

Printed in the United States of America
SC-R-3

Library of Congress Cataloging-in-Publication Data

Hill, Deborah J.
    School days, fun days : creative ways to use humor in the
classroom / by Deborah J. Hill ; illustrated by David R. Caperton.
        p.   cm.
    ISBN 0-398-05862-8
    1. Teacher-student relationships.   2. Humor in education.
3. Teaching.   I. Title.
LB1033.H495   1993
371.1'02'0207 — dc20
                                                                93-7241
                                                                CIP

INTRODUCTION

Everyone agrees it's important to have a sense of humor. Yet students have always been left to their own devices to develop the humor skills that become so important later in life. The purpose of this book is to propose ways to teach students to cultivate their own unique sense of humor and to develop joke technique as a creative skill.

Children learn from everything they do. To young students, everything is an adventure, with the exception, of course, of "yukki stuff" like homework. The good news for teachers is that little humans are innately curious. They want to learn as much as you want to teach them. The only obstacle is that young students also want learning to be fun, or they'll resist it like a bowl full of beets or anything else adults claim is "good" but which somehow doesn't smell quite right.

Students don't have to see school as a place to learn, in the same way they don't have to think of dinner as a time to eat nutritious vegetables. School days can be fun days, full of activity and surprise.

As every teacher knows, in order to get to the heart of any lesson, it is first necessary to review some introductory material. In this tradition, the first chapters of *School Days, Fun Days* examine some of the fundamentals before getting to the "good stuff," like the funny jokes. By fundamentals I mean the development of a sense of humor, the psychology of laughter, and the sociology of laughter in groups. The research for this introductory material includes many interviews with professional comedians as well as much reading of stuffy reports. I hope I have made the basics as palatable as possible. If not, feel free to skip to the zingers in subsequent chapters.

The Interpretation of Humor

There is virtually nothing in life that does not have its humorous side. Still, some people feel there are certain things we must never joke about—like teachers and the education of our youth. At no time does this book mean to make light of important issues, not even in the jokes about principals in Chapter 4. . . .

Students are most receptive to learning when it comes in the spirit of excitement, the kind of excitement laughter often generates. In the classroom, it is the teacher who sets the mood of the day. Your smiles and laughter establish classroom playfulness and the fun of the learning environment.

Most humor has its time and place, its appropriate context and precisely timed moment. *School Days, Fun Days* offers ideas and insights into the world of humor studies with suggested exercises to supplement the text.

One more thing about the interpretation of a humorous event. All of us have a unique sense of humor. No comedy can please all of the people all of the time, because there's no such thing as a joke that all people consider to be funny. The exercises in this book suggest jokes and humorous phrases to supplement individual lessons. Feel free to substitute these with your own quips or with jokes that are more relevant to your students.

CONTENTS

Introduction   v

Chapter 1—Developing a Sense of Humor   3

   I.   *Humor and Infancy*   3

        Laughter and Cognition   4

   II.   *Why Do We Laugh? The Psychology of Humor*   5

        The Meaning of Laughter   7

        Cruel and Polite Laughter   7

        People and Personalities   8

        Family and Upbringing   8

        The Measurement of Laughter   10

   III.   *Developing Humor Skills in the Classroom*   10

        Laughter and Memory Recall   11

Chapter 2—Fun and Games   13

   I.   *Play Time*   14

        Toys   14

        Preschool Play   15

        Kindergarten Play   16

        Lower Grade School (Grades 1–3)   16

        Upper Grade School (Grades 4–6)   17

        Junior High and High School Play   18

        Violence and Play   19

   II.   *Games*   20

        Exercise: The Money Game   20

        Sporting Games   21

        Teaching Good Sportsmanship   23

   III.   *Mind Games*   23

        Brain Teasers   23

        Riddles   24

        Puzzles   25

Chapter 3—Humor in the Classroom   26

   I.   *Allowable Laughter*   26
      Story Time   27
      Party Time   27
      Fun with Food   28

  II.   *Forbidden Laughter*   29
      Taboo Language   29
      Insults, Comebacks and Putdowns   30
      Racism and Sexism in Jokes   32
      Pranks   32
      Laughter, Stupidity and Sin   33

 III.   *The Role of the Class Clown*   34
      Games Students Play   35
      Name Games: Who's On First?   35
      Interruption   36
      Oh, really?!   36
      I'm Innocent   37
      You Said!   37
      How Should I Know?   38
      No One Here But Us Chickens   38

 IV.   *Disciplining the Class Clown*   39
      Be Brief, But Firm   39
      Do's and Don'ts   40

  V.   *Group Laughter*   40
      Group Glee   42
      Gender and Groups   42
      Effective Seating Plans   43

Chapter 4—The Teacher as Entertainer   45

   I.   *Role Model vs. Human Being*   45
      Developing a Comic Technique   46
      Teacher Stress   47

  II.   *Joking Relationships*   49
      Child-Parent   50
      Student-Teacher   52
      Parent-Teacher   53
      Student-Student   54

Teacher-Teacher 55

Teacher-Administrator 56

Chapter 5—Teaching Creativity 58

   I.   *Humor and Creativity* 58

      Inspiration 59

      The Joy of Accomplishment 60

  II. *Supplies* 60

      Clay 60

      Paper 61

        • Snowflakes 61

        • Paper spirals 62

        • Collages 62

 III. *Humor in Arts and Crafts* 63

      Mirror Drawings 63

      Comics and Cartoons 63

      Caricatures 64

      Clown Art 65

      Monster Necklaces and Ropes 65

      Trees 65

      Mobiles 66

      Thinking Caps 66

      Greeting Cards 66

      Book Writing 67

      Bulletin Boards 67

 IV. *Cleanup Fun* 68

Chapter 6—Laughter and Anxiety 69

  Schoolroom Anxiety 69

      I.   *The Physiology of Laughter* 70

      II. *Humor and Test Anxiety* 71

      III. *Fear of Public Speaking* 74

      IV. *Crisis Humor* 76

Chapter 7—Language and Laughter 80

  I. *Pronunciation* 81

      Alliteration 81

      Onomatopaeia 82

      Homonyms 82

Homophones 83

Accents 83

II. *Mispronunciations* 84

Hyperpronunciations 84

Spoonerisms 85

Malapropisms 85

Tongue Twisters 85

Speech Defects 86

III. *Humor and Language* 86

Grammar and Syntax 86

Personification 87

Fun with Poetry 88

IV. *Language and Meaning* 88

Semantics 88

Etymology 89

Eponyms 89

Acronyms 89

Abbreviations 90

Chapter 8—The Ambiguity of Language 91

I. *The Humor of Double-Entendre* 91

Oxymoron 93

Synonyms 94

Euphemisms 94

Cliches and Sayings 95

Similes 96

Metaphors 97

It Goes Without Saying 99

Making Sense of Nonsense 100

II. *Non-Verbal Communication* 101

Body Language 101

Gesture Jokes 101

Contagious Smiles and Laughter 102

Chapter 9—Anatomy of a Joke 103

I. *Joke Construction* 103

Setups and Surprise 104

Cue the Listener 105

Punchlines 105
Exaggeration and Understatement 106
Contrast 107
Conciseness 107
Playfulness 109
II. *Joke Formats* 110
Puns 110
Tom Swifties 110
Sports Jokes 111
Competition Jokes 111
Light Bulb Jokes 112
Elephant Jokes 113
Good News/Bad News 113
Tall Tales and White Lies 114
III. *Cracking Jokes* 115
Memorizing Jokes 115
Projection 116
Intonation and Emphasis 116
Speech Clarity 116
Naturalness 117
Timing 117
Establishing Rapport 117
Hooks 118
Save Lines 118
Going Too Far 118
Positive Feedback 119
Teaching Joke Etiquette 120
Chapter 10—The Joy of Drama 121
I. *Comedy Style and Technique* 121
Slapstick 122
Farce 122
Parody 123
Satire 123
Irony and Wit 123
Eirons and Alazons 124
Commedia dell'arte 125

	Vaudeville	125
	Anecdotes	126
II.	*It's Show Time!*	126
	Impersonations	126
	Clowning Around	127
	Pantomime	127
	Improvisation	128
	Puppet Fun	128
	Making Puppets	129
	Puppet Show Time	130
III.	*Simulation Learning*	130
	Fashion Show Fun	131
	Celebrity Look-Alike Contest	131
	Music Videos	132
Chapter 11—Computer Fun		133
I.	*Computer Technology 101*	134
	Computers	134
	Peripherals, Optionals and Attachments	135
	Monitors	136
	Printers	137
	Disk Drives	137
	Disk Operating Systems	137
II.	*Memory*	138
	Bits and Bytes	138
	Computer Memory Capacity	139
	Memory Storage and Retrieval	139
III.	*Working with the Computer*	140
	Shopping for a Computer	140
	Computer Maintenance in the Classroom	141
	What Can Go Wrong?	143
IV.	*Computer Programs*	143
	Software, Hardware and Firmware	143
	Educational Software Programs	144
	Multi-Media	146
	Virtual Reality	146
	Shopping for Software	147

Selected Fun Software 147
Software Manufacturers 149
Public Domain Software Companies 150

Chapter 12—Environmental Fun 151

I. *What's So Funny About the Environment?* 152

II. *Environmental Games We Should Play* 154

III. *Field Trips: Fun in Your Own Back Yard* 155
Take a Field Trip to the Woods 155
Take a Trip to a Tree Farm 155
Take a Trip to a Plant Store 155
Take a Field Trip to a Fish Hatchery 155

IV. *Fun With Our Changing Seasons* 156
Set Up a Recycling System in Your Room 156
Build a Compost Pile 157
Have a "Fix It" Day 157
Make Seasonal Bulletin Boards 157

V. *Appreciating the Animal World* 157

VI. *Organic Cooking, New Lessons in Home Economics* 159

VII. *Whole Earth Handicrafts: Making History Come Alive* 159

VIII. *Environmental Fun with Local Experts* 160

IX. *Environmental Safety in the Classroom* 160

X. *The Importance of Fun in the Natural World* 162

SCHOOL DAYS, FUN DAYS

Chapter 1

DEVELOPING A SENSE OF HUMOR

The sense of humor is what makes you laugh at something
that would make you angry if it happened to you.

Anonymous

I. HUMOR AND INFANCY

From our earliest existence, happiness is associated with good physical and mental health. People think of infants who laugh and smile as good babies, while crybabies are viewed as sick or disobedient.

Whatever a baby's disposition, the first smile usually appears around the first to third week after birth. This first smile is associated with the pleasurable experience of feeding and feeling safe. New babies also smile at funny faces, surprising noises and new objects, as long as these are not seen as frightening or dangerous.

As infants grow older, smiles become increasingly broad until the

3

third or fourth month when babies learn to laugh. Infants who smile early in life usually develop an early laugh as well. Throughout the first year of development, infants will smile at peek-a-boo games and tickling.

As infants acquire more information in their memories, they begin to smile in recognition of familiar faces and objects. Throughout life, the smile of recognition continues to express the pleasure of discovering something familiar, as when we unexpectedly see former possessions.

At the same time infants develop humorous expressions, they are learning what makes people close to them laugh. They also learn what feels good, what makes mommy and daddy angry and what gets the most attention. In these early months, poopy diapers, sleepless nights and overturned formula bottles test the patience and sense of humor of even the most loving parents. Nevertheless, parental smiles and laughter help to satisfy the infant's constant need for attention and love.

Laughter and Cognition

Developmental psychologists have proposed specific stages in the development of cognition, the acquisition of knowledge. According to the Swiss psychologist, Jean Piaget (1896–1980), cognitive development begins at the "prenatal" stage, the period from conception to birth. During "infancy" (birth to 18 months), babies learn to move, make social attachments and develop a rudimentary language.

Piaget explained that during "early childhood" (18 months to age six) language is established, sex is typed, group play begins and the child becomes ready for school. During "late childhood" (ages 6–13), children continue to develop adult cognitive skills. "Adolescence" (ages 13–20) begins with puberty and ends with "maturity." Mature individuals reach the highest levels of cognition, becoming independent of parents and engaging in sexual relations.

Cognitive development is related both to a child's internal processes (feelings, intentions and expectations) and their external situation. Piaget explained that children begin their lives as "naive realists," believing everything they see to be reality. As the child matures, they match new knowledge with old information until they are able to perceive the difference between reality and fantasy during the second year.

How important is a child's ability to fantasize, and what does this cognitive skill have to do with the sense of humor? The answer is, very important. Many psychologists believe that "fantasy assimilation," the ability to perceive the difference between fantasy and reality, is necessary before a child can perceive an event as humorous. In other words, once children feel comfortable naming objects in the real world, they can "play," renaming things for fun.

The ability to interpret things as humorous is expanded as language development progresses. By the time a child enters school, they have already begun to comprehend that words have multiple and ambiguous meanings. Throughout the school years, they will come increasingly closer to adult abilities in the interpretation and expression of humor.

II. WHY DO WE LAUGH? THE PSYCHOLOGY OF HUMOR

People laugh at so many things. We laugh at the incongruous, the unexpected, the unusual, the ridiculous, the ironical or clever. We laugh at nonsense and stupidity, at exaggeration and deformity and at the grotesque. We also laugh when we're happy, relieved or even when we feel hostile. But what is the sense of humor really about?

The word "humor" comes from the Latin word for liquid, a reference to the body's four body fluids. The earliest psychologists believed the human body was divided into four fluids: blood, phlegm, choler and black bile. Too much of one humor over another supposedly determined the disposition of a person which could be sanguine (happy), phlegmatic (sluggish), choleric (bad-tempered) or melancholy (depressed). Medieval medical prescriptions sought to rebalance body fluids believed to cause the physical and psychological discomfort. Bloodlettings, for example, might cure overly sanguine patients, if doctors didn't kill them with another remedy first.

Some have suggested that laughter and crying were the most primitive forms of communication. Laughing and crying may have communicated basic emotions like happiness and sadness before a more complex language system evolved.

Evolutionists believe the sense of humor developed as a survival mechanism. In fact, laughter helps us to cope by allowing us to endure painful thoughts about failure and death. People also laugh to protect true emotions, as an aggressive expression, or to defend during attack.

Sigmund Freud proposed that some kinds of jokes are "harmless," causing joy by allowing us to return to infantile nonsense and absurdity. Truly humorous events possess an ageless quality. No matter how old or young, most of us laugh at "infantile" forms of humor like The Three Stooges, Oliver and Hardy, the Muppets and Pee Wee Herman.

Sigmund Freud presented the psychoanalytic theory of humor in his influential book, *Wit and Its Relation to the Unconscious* (1905). In it he related the sense of humor to different stages of psychosexual development. When children begin to perceive taboos related to things like sex and elimination, they develop a "joke facade" which disguises forbidden subjects. Freudians also believe we laugh at things we fear, including unresolved childhood conflicts.

Have you ever heard a joke in the morning, but found yourself unable to remember it a few hours later? Freudians believe the unconscious mind represses jokes that contain socially unacceptable sexual or aggressive messages.

Abraham Maslow's "hierarchy of priority" helps explain why we are more likely to laugh at certain times over others. According to Maslow, humans must fulfill basic physical and psychological needs before they can experience playful moods. Physical needs take highest priority, followed by safety, love, belonging and self-esteem. Not everyone behaves according to Maslow's hierarchy, but it is usually true that people are less likely to smile and laugh when they are physically or emotionally uncomfortable.

Like many forms of communication, laughter may be either a *voluntary* emotion produced at will, or an *involuntary* emotion. Involuntary laughing can be forced by drugs like marijuana or "laughing gas," used in some dentist offices. Involuntary laughter can also be a symptom of disease as when a mentally ill person cannot control hysterical behavior. Laughter may be involuntary during periods of extreme fatigue when humans become "punchy" or silly even when nothing particularly funny is happening. In addition to an emotional response, laughter may be a *reflex reaction,* as when the skin is tickled.

We also laugh at events we can relate to at a specific stage in life, provided an event is not too painfully truthful. Thus, we laugh at a falling clown because we can identify with a clumsy being; but we are not amused if we actually fall ourselves, especially if others are laughing at us.

Even when we think we know ourselves, few of us are so knowledgeable about our own psychology that we can explain why we think something is funny every time we laugh. Sometimes we laugh even when something is not humorous. We smile and laugh to hide true feelings, or

inhibit amusement for social reasons, the way we learn to control ourselves from laughing when someone farts in church.

Some attribute our constant search for laughter as an indication of our
inability to communicate directly. This requires us to communicate
about taboo subjects indirectly through jokes. Laughter in modern man
is a complex psycho-social phenomena, and thankfully something that
brings enjoyment to the human spirit. Whatever the cause of the laughter,
it is good that the mood of modern classrooms allows us to be more
expressive and to enjoy the lighter side of life as we teach and learn.

The Meaning of Laughter

For all we know about the psychology of humor, the meaning of
laughter is amazingly imprecise. Humorous expressions have been
associated with emotions as varied as friendliness and hostility, decep-
tion or nostalgia, insecurity as well as inner peace. Like other forms of
non-verbal communication, the interpretation of smiling and laughter is
complex, depending on the context of the situation.

Smiles and laughter, like other forms of non-verbal communication,
convey imprecise messages. Literary laughter allows us to recognize a
witch (he he he), Santa Claus (ho ho ho), or hillbillies (haw haw haw).
Stylized laughter can communicate other messages besides humor as
when as accusing "A–HA!" means, "I caught you," or a sarcastic "Ha ha"
(very funny) signifies "I don't think that was very amusing."

Cruel and Polite Laughter

Some people interpret pre-school humor as "cruel" because young
children are uninhibited about making fun of the world around them. In
fact, most children do not understand acceptable joking behavior until
around age six or seven, when they begin school.

Grade school students sometimes laugh at jokes because they want to
join in on the fun, even when they do not understand a joke. This is not
polite laughter, however. Very young students do not yet understand
how to empathize with other people, how to laugh politely when something isn't funny, or how to inhibit laughter that might hurt others.

People and Personalities

Laughter, like other behaviors, is internalized by the personal experiences of the individual. Our unique personalities are a result of upbringing and life experiences, causing some of us to be impulsive, and others to be careful. Some people become optimists, others pessimists. Some develop a positive self-concept, while others go through life disliking themselves. Whatever our mood or disposition, the unique qualities of our personality determine how we perceive, enjoy and produce humor.

Already in the crib, a baby's disposition indicates the child's sense of humor throughout life. Some babies learn that smiles get them what they want most—the attention and care of adults. Other babies discover that crying is more effective. Some babies are born with a laughing disposition, while others are born with opposite inclinations.

Psychologists sometimes explain personality differences by dividing children into "impulsive" and "reflective" types. Impulsive students tend to react to humorous events quickly and expressively, but may miss subtleties perceived by more reflective students who prefer to laugh to themselves. Reflective students usually develop a "drier," more intellectual sense of humor, while the typical extrovert prefers clowning, slapstick and down-to-earth jokes.

Studies have shown that people with positive self-images develop a stronger and healthier sense of humor than those who do not. Ironically, many professional comics admit it was low self-esteem that made them seek out the love and laughter of the stage.

Personality studies show that conservative students are more likely to prefer "safe" jokes, while liberals tend to prefer more adventurous jokes. "Divergent thinkers" are better able to make more unusual associations about events and ideas than "convergent" or linear thinkers. In addition, divergent thinkers usually tell jokes more frequently.

Family and Upbringing

There is no sure formula that determines why one child develops a healthy sense of humor while another does not. Some children develop an acute sense of humor as they compete for parental attention. Other children become grave and earnest for the same reason.

Nevertheless, a youngster's sense of humor is influenced by the mood of the home. Parental attitudes about laughter, what parents consider to be funny, and whether or not the child has positive or negative experiences with family laughter will influence the child's sense of humor at school. Usually, the child who enjoys a healthy joking relationship with parents and siblings also develops a healthy joking relationship with classmates and teachers.

Children sometimes develop a sense of humor as a coping mechanism when there is conflict in the home. In some cases, dominant rival siblings intimidate a child, making them introverted, fearful and serious. Unwanted children or children born in former marriages sometimes become the victims of derisive laughter. In dysfunctional families, the children themselves may be the ones who generate hostile jokes with unwanted step-relatives.

Parents sometimes make the mistake of not taking childish concerns seriously, laughing at children's attempts to express themselves or making light of their emotions or problems. Other times, adults do not respond to a child's attempts at joking because they're too busy, or because a child's demand on a parent's time can be impossible to fulfill. Parents normally laugh at the cute things children do. However, if children believe they are being ridiculed rather than admired, they can become overly sensitive to laughter.

The sense of humor may depend on the position of a child among other siblings. Firstborns are said to be more gregarious, while babies are shyer. The middle child is supposed to be best adjusted psychologically. However, children often defy rules about behavior. Individuals often rise above their family circumstance, developing a healthy sense of humor even when family life is unpleasant. Others become somber even when other family members are lively and animated.

How parents react to children during toilet training, about the use of taboo words, or to questions about sex will influence a child's sense of humor as well. Many jokes prove we feel anxious about taboo subjects such as sex education. There's the old joke about the child who asked his parents where he was from. After listening to a lengthy explanation of the birds and the bees, the child replied, "I thought I was from New Jersey." For some children, sexual or scatological jokes offer socially acceptable ways to relieve tension or anxiety about these normally forbidden subjects.

The Measurement of Laughter

Experimental psychologists have had moderate success measuring the laughter response. Part of the problem is that experts don't agree about how to test the sense of humor. Among other things, different results are influenced by the theoretical approach of the psychologist and the disposition of the individual or the group at the time the test is given. There are also many psycho-social variables including upbringing, personality, gender, and age.

In spite of the difficulties in the measurement of laughter, psychologists have developed special *Mirth Response Tests* to examine the laughter of groups and individuals. The Mirth Response Test allows psychologists to evaluate school-age children by using cartoons or verbal jokes which are then rated on a specific scale. More precise measurements are achieved using the *Facial Action Code* (*FAC*) which interprets facial movements and the emotions associated with them.

Mirth Response Tests present problem-solving tasks involving some incongruity or absurdity. While clowning is especially humorous to young people, psychologists have devoted most of their attention to the study of verbal and visual humor. Since formal testing is not as easy with preschoolers, the humor of very young students is usually measured by observation alone.

III. DEVELOPING HUMOR SKILLS IN THE CLASSROOM

Humor in the classroom was not taken seriously until recently. Now, more and more universities are including humor studies as a formal course of study. This is particularly true in psychology departments but also of the education curriculum. A growing number of seminars and classes are now available for hopeful stand-up comedians as well, some of whom work full time as teachers.

This growing interest in humor is an indication of North America's awareness of the importance of humor in our society. Television situation comedy is an integral part of family life, and the names of many stand-up comics are household words. Many physicians use humor as a part of recuperative therapy, and educators are taking a more active role in developing a healthy sense of humor among students.

There are a number of pitfalls for teachers who hope to help students to develop humor skills in the classroom. Students sometimes hide the fact that being smart is important to them by joking about being stupid or insulting intelligence. In many grade school jokes the brightest students become "geeks" and "brains." The smartest students may get the best grades, but they are often viewed as less desirable socially, even made fun of by more popular, stylish students.

One reason students want to show they are smart is to impress the teacher. When teachers show that they are humans who make mistakes and can laugh at themselves, students understand that failure is as much a part of the classroom as success. Students also learn that school is a place where the most important thing is to try one's best.

Laughter and Memory Recall

Psychoanalysts believe some information goes into the long-term memory, but is repressed in the unconscious mind, making it less accessible. Jokes are often quickly forgotten because they are associated with socially unacceptable sexual or aggressive events, or fears related to childhood conflicts. Because jokes are so closely associated with the memory and emotions, they provide a perfect memory-recall exercise. While humor is never a substitute for substance, it can certainly make knowledge acquisition less painful.

There are also advantages to cultivating the sense of humor in school. As students learn to develop their sense of humor, they may be improving their ability to remember information. The ability to recall information is one of the most important skills students must learn to succeed in school. Much of the information that enters the short-term memory is quickly forgotten. This is because students do not perceive information as important enough to retain for long-term recall. When students associate learning with the positive emotional experience laughter brings, they are more likely to remember subject matter and to recall it fondly.

Repetition is one of the most important factors in converting new data into long-term memory. Psycho-linguists note that oft-repeated information is the last thing to deteriorate in the aging brain. Over time, people who lose language abilities most often retain information like their names as well as data associated with emotionally important events.

In some cases, students may not know how to convert short-term data into long-term memory banks. Professional comics know that the more they retell their jokes, the better able they are to recall them under pressure. In the same way, students will be better able to recall subject matter under exam-taking pressure if they have repeated the subject matter enough times.

Chapter 2

FUN AND GAMES

For what do we live, but to make sport for our neighbours, and laugh at them in our turn?

Mr. Bennet in Jane Austen's *Pride and Prejudice*

Young students are constantly looking for something new and fun. They look for diversion during free time, before or after recess, on rainy days, or in between more serious lessons when they hope for something fun before work resumes. Every day, students hope that fun and games will make school a playful experience.

At the same time, few among us do not fear the onset of playful behavior and the chaos play implies. In fact, play does not have to be raucus. Play can be quietly amusing or mildly enjoyable, at least that's what I've heard.

I. PLAY TIME

Play is defined as anything we do to amuse ourselves including sports and games. Play is frivolous and mischievous; it is infantile, fun and sometimes silly. More importantly, play is a learning experience, not only because students share knowledge when they play, but because playing and sharing teaches important social skills. Experts now realize that much of our adult social behavior is learned during childhood play.

Toys

While much childhood play depends on the imagination, today's kids want lots of toys. While some toys are generic, most are age-specific and task oriented. No matter what the age of the child, the best toys are ones that are safe, durable, interesting, challenging and fun. Optimally, toys should also develop skills suited to the child's personality.

Infants prefer toys they can reach for, grab and touch. Infants also like stimulating toys, usually ones that make sounds and that feel good; things they can bite as they endure teething.

As soon as babies sit up they want to start building things. Babies like to pile blocks and rings on top of one another. Rolling toys help them make the transition from crawling to walking.

Around 18 months babies become interested in colorful picture books, taking delight in simple drawings of familiar objects. Young children are also soothed by simple bedtime stories.

Preschool toys are often miniature models of things found in the adult world; things like dish sets, trucks, little furniture and so forth. Preschoolers continue playing with building blocks. They also like to model clay and do simple arts and crafts projects with paint, crayons or other easy-to-use materials. As preschoolers experience fantasy assimilation, they befriend stuffed animals and dolls as friends and playmates, and begin to imitate creatures in the natural world when they play.

Preschoolers also like to play with violent toys, much to the dismay of most parents. While some believe that violent toys like tomahawks, ray guns and rubber knives actually teach children to control their violent impulses in socially acceptable ways, others believe violent toys teach children to become desensitized to violence. Nevertheless, when it comes to toys, kids know what they want. One mother who refused to buy her son a toy gun said she gave up one evening after he carved a gun out of a piece of cheese. Other kids who decide they want to play violent games use sticks or other makeshift weapons, which doesn't make most of them mass murderers.

By the time students reach the first grade they prefer toys that might better qualify as games. They understand rules, they know how to share, and they like to play with friends. Role-playing games allow students to dress up and make-believe. Later, grade schoolers want more complex toys such as chemistry sets, toy rockets, and stamp collections.

Preschool Play

One of the things that distinguishes preschoolers from elementary school children is that preschoolers need guidance in their play, asking adults to help them occupy their free moments. Fantasy plays an important role in preschool play. Preschoolers find it humorous to invent games, amusing themselves with inner fantasies as they hum and talk to themselves.

Preschoolers are in a discovery period in which they find pleasure in seeing and touching new things. Like infants, preschoolers laugh at funny faces and silly adults. Preschoolers also enjoy being chased, as long as they don't feel threatened by the chaser.

Preschoolers begin to imitate adults in their play. Infantile role playing is a fundamental part of the socialization process that precedes school. During these formative years, young children play games around the roles of mommy and daddy, as well as career roles like doctor or nurse. Some of the skills developed in these early role-playing games evolve into the individual's joke-telling style.

Particularly after the age of two, language begins to play an important role in children's fun and games. As preschoolers develop their language abilities, they begin to experiment with words, sometimes inventing nonsense words that sound funny, or rhyming words for fun.

Preschoolers experiment with their vocal cords, changing pitch, trying to imitate sounds, making noises, singing, stretching the lips or playing with the tongue while talking. For the next several years, children will laugh at the sounds of animals and funny voices. Preschoolers take great delight in listening to stories when adult readers use exaggerated impersonations of storybook characters.

Kindergarten Play

Kindergarten children (usually age 5) begin to learn to play in groups, to share, and to obey their new surrogate parent, the teacher. At this early age, kindergarteners are spontaneous, sometimes selfish, affectionate and anxious to please.

Kindergarteners love the teacher. They want to be noticed, to be rewarded and praised. Five-year-olds are also afraid of this new world. They may burst into tears as they experience new frustrations during play including bigger kids, unfair pushers or playground meanies.

Like newborns in the baby wards, kindergarteners are greatly influenced by those around them. One crybaby, or one scream after a clap of thunder, can start a crying panic.

At the same time, kindergarteners can jump into a happy time at a moment's notice, following the lead of the teacher. Suggest a fun game to a group of kindergarteners, and they are sure to clap their hands in cheerful enthusiasm as you guide them to a better mood.

Lower Grade School (Grades 1-3)

By the time children reach elementary school, they have had hundreds of game-playing experiences with other children; game experiences which determine how students will behave in your classroom, even in non-game situations. School play teaches responsible good behavior and self-reliance.

During the first year of school, students derive much of their pleasure from play and the freedom it represents. Like preschoolers, younger students enjoy fantasy and make-believe, role playing, toys, bike riding, ball games and other sports. Elementary school students can play alone and laugh to themselves or play with others, caring much less than adolescents about getting wet, muddy or dirty.

The main difference between kindergarten students and first graders is that the older children have learned to accept the discipline and routine of the classroom. In fact, during the first three years of grade school, students rely on routines to make them feel secure that they are doing the right thing. First through third graders are still anxious to please the teacher. They work well in groups, are willing to share and help, and still maintain that spontenaeity that makes young children so endearing.

As they mature, grade school children will experience more delight in play that offers greater challenges. Students in the lower grades find pleasure in make-believe role-playing games, in the challenges of new toys, the competition of board games or physical sports. Popular grade school play includes hide and seek, tag, hopscotch, jacks or marbles, London Bridge, ring-around-the-roses, Red Rover or Simon says, catch, musical chairs and mother-may-I.

As elementary school students master their speech muscles, they begin to experiment with tongue twisters and secret languages like Pig Latin. Elementary school children also memorize riddles and humorous poems as well as defensive comebacks like, *"sticks and stones may break my bones but words can never hurt me."*

Upper Grade School (Grades 4–6)

The fourth grade, for most students, is a transitional period to the upper grades. Students feel more secure in school, and clowning and horseplaying are more likely to take place in the classroom as students begin to challenge the authority of adults. Fourth graders have not yet been completely accepted by fifth and sixth graders, so part of their new concerns have to do with an intense desire to be grown up.

Fourth graders like to challenge their minds and bodies. They enjoy more complex puzzles and brain teasers than the simple riddles enjoyed in earlier grades. They are also able to play more complex games like football and baseball. Around age 10 students become more independent, and while they still work well in groups, they prefer reading to themselves over being read to by a storyteller.

Fifth and sixth graders are the school leaders. Physically, they are larger. They are more fashion conscious as they follow the fads of older students, and peer pressure becomes keener. Students become much more conscious of self, and belonging to the right group becomes much more important.

By the upper grades, individuals are also much more aware of their physical and academic strengths and weaknesses, and are either proud or unhappy about their abilities. This means they are less likely to follow teacher initiatives that might make them look foolish in front of their most significant others, their classmates.

Fifth and sixth graders are more likely to be mischief-makers and pranksters. Getting into trouble may even be part of their idea of fun.

While students always want to please their teachers, by the sixth grade, they begin to see themselves as the good guys and teachers and parents as a potential enemy, the adult, the inhibiter, and someone who doesn't always understand.

Junior High and High School Play

As children approach puberty, they become increasingly curious about sex and procreation. This new preoccupation is reflected in increasing numbers of jokes with sexual content during the junior high school years. The following joke switches the stereotype.

> **A principal saw a group of junior high students huddled and whispering and demanded to know what they were doing.**
> **"We're telling dirty jokes," one of them said.**
> **"Oh," said the principal. "For a minute, I thought you were praying."**

Pubescent students will laugh at anything with sexual implications, and for some of them, everything has sexual potential. Junior high school boys, for example, may find a banana enormously funny because they are more conscious of penises and erections, and also embarrassed about their new sexuality.

Everyone notices that junior high school girls are more mature than the boys. Many jokes about junior high boys make light of the fact that they haven't quite caught up with the girls yet. For example, there was the junior high school boy who spotted a pretty girl and said, *"I don't like girls yet, but when I do, she's the one I'm going for."*

Junior high school joking begins to resemble adult humor. As junior high students acquire more vocabulary and life experience, their jokes become more complex and sophisticated. Junior high students prefer memorized and personal anecdotes to one-liners and riddles. By the seventh and eighth grades students have developed an individual joke-telling style.

As far as play is concerned, junior high boys are more likely to roughneck, pushing each other around, accusing one another of everything from homosexuality to the unspeakable act of kissing a girl. Bragging includes exaggerations about sexual exploits, the size of the genitalia, and ability to master any moment.

Junior high is both an exciting and frightening time for students. They are likely to be at multiple achievement levels within the same classroom. They begin to look like adults, but their social behavior is often crude, clumsy, sometimes rude and often rough around the edges. It is the junior high school teacher who will have a special place in heaven, since they need a great deal of patience to get students ready for the greater academic rigors and physical demands of high school.

While the freshman year is frightening for its newness, by the time students reach the tenth grade, they are truly young adults. They have fewer fears in life, and begin to openly challenge ideas and people they disagree with. Challenges in play most often take place around school-organized athletic activities. Students feel part of the group identity of the school and winning and losing as a school becomes ever more important.

High school games are similar to those we play as adults; strategic board games, computer games, video arcade games as well as advanced puzzles or brain teasers which challenge new skills in mathematics and other subjects.

"Fooling around" takes on a whole new meaning for high school students. At some point, Spin-the-bottle and Post Office replace Tag and Hopscotch as favorite games to play.

What high school students do fear is new relationships, especially ones that involve sex. Jokes help relieve some of the anxiety that comes with a fear of rejection.

> "Sally's not like other girls," Joey said.
> "How so?"
> "She likes me."

> "A lot of girls don't want to go steady," Barry said.
> "How do you know?"
> "I've asked them."

Violence and Play

Saturday morning cartoons are full of creatures bonking each other on the head. Cartoon violence is a combination of what adults think children like, and what kids actually want. While children may not be naturally violent, they seem to enjoy slapstick in cartoons and films.

Children learn from imitation, and some will bring cartoon and comic hero violence to the playground. Between Kung Fu, Rambo and the Ninja Turtles, it's surprising there are any kids left alive on the playgrounds at all. Teachers on recess duty sometimes must explain to children the difference between make-believe violence and the real thing, although a swift kick to the upper jaw by a fellow student is usually lesson enough.

II. GAMES

While play implies general frivolity, game usually refers to structured kinds of play. Games have formalized rules about acceptable playing behavior. Games also have criteria such as point systems for progressing, losing and winning. The object of every game is to WIN! Teaching games means teaching how to be a humble winner and how to be a graceful loser, a skill few of us master in the end.

Students need discipline and rules. They want to be wild, but they seek rules of a game, even the spontaneous rules of unstructured play which are often made up as the game goes along. Once the guidance is given, however, students can be relied upon to bring an active imagination and sense of adventure to a playful assignment like the one below.

Exercise: The Money Game

Children love to spend money once they learn what it means to earn it, save it and count it. In this exercise, fun items are priced according to a value determined by the students. Fun things to buy include inexpensive toys or snacks. Buy several similar things and price them slightly differently, depending on advantages one product has over another. Put some items on sale. Once prices have been set, students are given periodic assignments to complete in exchange for play money. Once students have some money they can decide what they would like to do with it. Here are some of the choices:

1) They can spend it right away, exchanging it for M&M's or crayons or some other treat. If they choose to do this, discuss with them the value of each article and make sure they understand what a "bargain" is. If some items don't sell, put them on sale and see what students think about the lower prices.

2) Some students may not want anything you have for sale. These students can open a bank account and save their money until there is something in the store they want, or until they have enough

money to afford an item that is too expensive for their current budget.

Sporting Games

The purpose of sporting games is twofold. Not only do athletic games teach students how to share and play by rules as a team, they also allow students to exercise while challenging their physical abilities. At the same time, balls and bats are desirable toys. While pens and pencils may be fun, you can't kick them around on a playing field or score a goal like you can with a puck.

Students are compelled to touch and throw and kick anything that resembles a ball, which means you need to keep your equipment in some central place, locked away until it's time to play. Students also need to understand that the purpose of sporting games is more than a mere annihilation of the other team. Yes, we want to cream our rivals, but there's more to it than that. At the very least, playing games teaches responsibility, even as we stampede the field with hockey sticks and baseball bats like a band of ravaging Vikings.

One way to teach responsibility is to give each team player a job. Someone needs to carry equipment to the field, someone must dispurse equipment, and someone else should collect and count equipment at the end of the game. There are team captains and co-captains, someone to keep score and a few people to officiate the game. No matter how large a team is, everyone should have a job and understand that the team depends on everyone doing their share.

There is nothing quite so challenging as dividing a class into teams. Popular kids and athletes inevitably find it fun to team up against the nerds, while teachers try to divide talents as fairly as possible. Rotating captains gives everyone a chance at leadership, and avoids the problem of alienating the athletically disinclined students who would rather read *War and Peace* than have to play another game of wiffle ball.

Before they storm the playing field, students must learn the rules of the game. Rules should be as clear as possible to avoid mid-game disputes or feelings of unfairness. However, no matter how many rules you devise, something will occur that has never happened before on any playing field in history, and some rules will have to be devised on the spot. Appointing fairness officials teaches students to deal with problems among their peers.

As game time approaches, communicate information to your students at some central locale. They will want to see a list of team members, the time and date of the game and any other information important to the safe and semi-organized execution of the event. To make announcements especially fun, roust enthusiasm by featuring the event as the "game of the decade" or as an "unprecedented, colossal, sporting event of the century."

Communication during a sporting event is likely to be reduced to cheek-popping whistle blowing, frantic arm waving and shouts unheard above the din of players. To avoid confusion, organize a communication system that allows captains to signal players, teammates to signal game plans and teachers to signal anybody.

In a short time it will be easy to cultivate a healthy rivalry among your students. Once you instill the murder instinct, give everyone an opportunity to exact revenge in the next game. Set up a tournament to keep score of the progress of ongoing sporting events. To make sure everyone wins a sports tournament, give awards based on playing excellence, good sportsmanship and fairness which are based on virtues rather than points accrued. Remember, of course, that winning isn't everything. Sex and money are important, too.

Students will enjoy playing games better if you give them a say in which games they will play. Since every class is different, take a survey and ask everyone about their favorite and least favorite games.

One way to make sports events more fun is to play a silly variation of a well-known game. For example:

Backwards baseball. Play baseball with the same rules as regular baseball, except right-handed players must use left hands and left-handers must use right hands.

Musical relays. Divide students into four teams. Have them race along an obstacle course that requires them to sing a silly song or perform a tongue twister rather than perform a physical task.

Water sausage baseball. Here's one for a hot day. Students play in the swimsuits, in teams of three players—a pitcher, catcher and batter. Use water sausages (water-filled balloons) instead of baseballs.

Frisbee football. Play football using a Frisbee instead of a football. Play this game away from trees or buildings where Frisbees can be lost.

Balloon volleyball. Play volleyball using a sturdy balloon instead of a volleyball. Points are lost for busting the balloon.

Bug race. Instead of having students run a race, organize an insect relay. Students form small groups of two or three people and catch their own insects (grasshoppers and beetles are better than wasps or flies). Make a tiny racetrack, and cheer your insects on. Anything that moves or moves the farthest in a one-minute time period is the winner. Please put insects back in the garden when finished.

Teaching Good Sportsmanship

Sometimes, superior laughter expresses triumph and victory, as when people deride opposing team members. Condescending laughter can be playful or hostile depending on the circumstances of the event. Good sportsmanship places rules of etiquette on the expression of hostility in games. Part of a coach's job is to teach enthusiastic fans or team players to limit the expression of hostile humor to socially acceptable levels. In other words, don't let anyone get killed.

III. MIND GAMES

Throughout the grade school years, students love to play mind games. Use them as a reward for good behavior or to make a fun transition between more structured lessons.

Brain Teasers

Anything that challenges the mind can be categorized as a brain teaser. There are many books of brain teaser exercises at your local bookstore and public library. To gage the level of your student's abilities, start with easier problems and move to more difficult challenges if students arrive at solutions too quickly.

Brain teasers teach students to challenge their mental abilities. Fun puzzles and riddles also teach test-taking skills. One typical type of brain teaser is the analogy. These set up comparisons that require students to understand relationships. For example:

Boston is to Massachusetts as _____ is to Egypt. (Cairo)
Green is to grass as _____ is to sky. (blue)

Another type of brain teaser is word math. In this game students add words to discover logical solutions. For example:

bees + flowers = _____ (honey)
chickens + barns + cows = (farms)

One way to challenge students with analogies is to require them to write their own.

Riddles

Riddles are jokes that pose questions which do not seem to have logical answers. Example:

Q: Why are brides unlucky on their wedding day?
A: Because they don't get to marry the best man.

Riddles prove that the listener is ignorant, unless he or she already knows the answer or can figure it out from the measly clues provided by the teller. Students enjoy riddles or "brain teasers" because they challenge minds with new cognitive abilities.

Riddles are language puzzles based on the ambiguity of words. Riddle ambiguity may be lexical (as when a single word has two meanings), phonological (as with synonyms), syntactical (using ambiguous word order) or semantic (confusing the meaning of words).

Exercise 1: *Answer the following simple riddles.*

What's the biggest pencil in the world?
Pennsylvania.

What's the longest word in the dictionary?
Smile—it ends with a mile

What's at the end of everything?
A "g".

What's the difference between here and there?
The letter "t".

What starts and ends with a T and is full of t.
A teapot.

What word becomes shorter by adding two letters?
The word short.

What word is pronounced wrong by everyone?
Wrong.

How is an island like the letter t?
Both are in the middle of water.

What has a foot but never wears shoes?
A mountain.

Exercise 2: *These riddles are slightly more difficult, but may be familiar to your students if they have friends or family members who like to share riddles.*

> **I have feet, but I can't walk (a yardstick)**
> **I have a mouth, but I can't eat (a cave)**
> **I have a tongue, but I can't speak (a shoe)**
> **I have legs, but I can't run (couch)**
> **I have hands, but I can't clap (a clock)**
> **I have ears, but I can't hear (corn)**
> **I have eyes, but I can't see (needles)**
> **I have keys, but no lock (a piano)**
> **I have legs, but I can't walk (a table)**
> **I have teeth, but I can't bite (a comb)**

Puzzles

Puzzle is a generic word that describes anything which causes uncertainty. Puzzles are solved by reasoning from hints or partial facts. Using limited information, the puzzle solver determines how to solve the mystery.

All riddles are also puzzles. However, most of us think of cross-word puzzles when we hear the word. Cross-word puzzles are a good way to teach students to work quietly and independently, and to use their reasoning abilities to solve a problem.

Exercise: *As an alternative to puzzles available in exercise books, let students create their own puzzles. To do this, write down twenty words, such as the week's vocabulary words, along with their definitions. These words will form the puzzle as words are crisscrossed with shared letters on graph paper or a grid you supply. Students can work alone or in teams.* Example:

> **as clear as glass (two words) = window pane**
> **use this to cut wood or to see (past tense) = saw**

s

window pane

w

When you complete crisscrossing all words, blacken empty blanks. Students can switch puzzles when they are finished to see if they have stumped their friends.

Chapter 3

HUMOR IN THE CLASSROOM

*If only men could be induced to laugh more they might hate
less, and find more serenity here on earth.*

Malcolm Muggeridge

I. ALLOWABLE LAUGHTER

Students soon learn when it is okay to laugh in the classroom. Teachers
tell jokes, funny things happen and sometimes it's just fun to work on
school projects. This section offers tips on ways to enhance those fun
times for your students.

This chapter is also about disruptive games students play and how to
avoid the antics of the class clown.

Story Time

Every child loves story time, especially when adults are animated and exciting. Here are a few basic reading tips to make your next reading session an exciting activity for your listeners.

1. Choose stories kids can relate to. These include:
   • Tales that reflect their everyday lives.
   • Stories that tell about characters in their favorite cartoons.
   • Fairy tales that allow students to enjoy the freedom of fantasy and creative imaginings.
2. Read slowly, and with dramatic expression; but not in a condescending or juvenile tone.
3. Stop often to ask students questions, to show them illustrations, to discuss the progress of the story, and to respond to their comments.
4. Use the active rather than the passive voice. Use action words with descriptive adjectives that conjure clear images of people, places and things.
5. Ask students to participate actively in the storytelling process. Have them describe characters and events in their own words, and let them guess what might happen next.
6. Instead of reading a story, make up a story as you go along, allowing students to introduce new characters, and to decide which way the action will turn.
7. Allow students to read to you. Younger students can read one or two simple words—older ones can take turns reading short phrases—or they can take the entire role of one characters, complete with a costume or prop.

Party Time

Holidays are special days for students, providing a diversion from routine chores. Some holidays give students a vacation from school. Others, like birthdays or barmitzvahs, call for special treatment from family and friends, including gift exchanges and yummy treats to eat.

Ideally, teaching children to anticipate and enjoy holidays teaches them to find joy in life. Were it not for holidays, all days would be the same and none of us would feel the same sense of progression as we do when we celebrate annual events. Holidays also instill in us a sense of nostalgia as one holiday event is repeated year after year, accumulating memories later recalled with fondness.

For many people, however, holidays are emotionally low times, full of disappointment and frustration. For some of these children, school may bring the best holiday memories they have.

While many things in life are cause for celebration, children learn a situation is joyful by watching those around them. If the teacher reacts to an event with animation, students usually follow suit.

National and religious holidays offer a chance for special lessons that teach students the meaning of annual celebrations and traditional fetes. Holiday lessons teach students the deeper meaning of rituals as well as the symbolism of things associated with the holiday.

One way to heighten the excitement of holidays is to anticipate them with playful, educational lessons several weeks before the event itself.

Of course, every day can't be a special day. Celebrations must be judiciously allocated so as not to wear out their unique quality and unusual extraordinary spirit.

Fun with Food

Students love to create and eat fun foods. Since eating is not normally part of the classroom routine, having fun with food is always a special classroom treat.

Fun foods are associated with the holidays. We associate marzipan with Christmas and candy corn with Halloween. Cake and ice cream are birthday treats, chocolate bunnies abound at Easter, and candy hearts fill store shelves around Valentine's Day. Many fun foods may be categorized as "junk food," less nutritious treats like candy apples and popcorn associated with circuses and fairs.

One way to have fun with food at school is to make edible creatures. Marshmellows and toothpicks and other bite-size candy can be used to make delicious tiny animals to eat in class or to take home.

Another way to have food fun is to use refreshments to teach students about ethnic cuisine. Each month students can learn about the food of a different country, sampling one or two dishes people around the world like to eat. Just as jokes find humor in contrast, students will find food lessons fun as they learn about cultural differences in the diets of people who eat differently than they do. Bulletin boards can supplement international lessons, helping students recognize where other countries are located in relation to home.

II. FORBIDDEN LAUGHTER

Much of the laughter we hear in the classroom is either "forbidden" or suppressed. There is a certain amount of naughtiness in schoolroom laughter, even if it is allowed, tolerated or even encouraged.

As soon as students learn what they're not supposed to joke about, they will want to joke about the forbidden. They'll tell you that *"bitch"* and *"bastard"* and *"ass"* are in the dictionary, for example, so it must be okay to say these words. Challenge is the nature of humor. Still, there is a joking ethos that can be instilled at an early age.

Taboo Language

Students laugh at taboo subjects for the same reason adults do; because these things make us anxious. In the preschool years, children laugh about potty training. Elementary school children, concerned about being smart in school, tell stupid-idiot jokes. During puberty, junior high and high school students disguise anxiety about sex in jokes about intercourse, promiscuity and genitalia.

As young boys experience anxiety about their first sexual experience and fears about homosexuality, they begin to call each other names like "queer" or "girl," or accuse each other of masturbating. Sexual information as well as misinformation is transmitted in jokes as friends share knowledge with less informed or less experienced school mates. Sex education is one way to help students to speak openly about the normally taboo subject of sex.

During the preschool and early school years, children begin to hear taboo words they do not understand. How adults react to taboo words will influence the child's attitude about reproducing this vocabulary. Children usually associate laughter with approval, which can reinforce negative behavior like repeating obscenities.

A bar of soap in the mouth was once the standard cure for a child who said a "bad" word. While most parents no longer react abusively, it is still necessary to teach very young children not to use certain words. As children grow older, we can explain to them that etiquette forbids specific words in certain situations for social, religious or moral reasons that are not always logical, even to adults. Teaching children to develop joke-telling skills includes the wholesome lesson that jokes do not need to include taboo language to be funny.

Parents and teachers socialize children to recognize linguistic taboos, many of which have double standards. While adults may curse among themselves, even in front of children, most will punish children for using the same language. Students eventually learn that people of the same age and sex use taboo language among themselves, but that people outside the group may be offended by "in-group" behavior. During the early school years students come to understand what words they should not use around adults or with members of the opposite sex.

Learning the rules of taboo language frustrates some young people who may use obscenities as a form of rebellion, to express anger, hostility and frustration, or to elicit laughter and attention. Many adults laugh the first time a child swears because the child doesn't understand what the obscenity means. (*"Hey Joey, tell Uncle Fred what you said this morning..."*)

If the child elicits laughter in several group situations, obscenities will seem like non-taboo words. This is especially true if parents seem to react positively to it, or by failing to punish the child who uses taboo or obscene language.

Insults, Comebacks and Putdowns

People tease each other throughout life. Preschoolers tease each other by pushing, stealing toys or game parts, or with simple one-word or one-scream insults. Sticking out the tongue is a form of non-verbal communication that serves as an effective insult before language skills are more advanced.

By the time students reach the first grade, they have memorized comebacks to ward off insults and aggressive linguistic confrontations. These early insults and comebacks are memorized like simple jokes and riddles. A typical conversation between young children anxious about being immature might sound something like this:

- Baby, baby!
- I know you are, but what am I?
- You're only five. Ha ha.
- What's that, your IQ?
- I'm rubber. Everything you say bounces off me and sticks to you.
- You wish.

Around the sixth grade, insulting becomes more complicated as language abilities are tested in increasingly complex social situations. Adolescents can feel extreme humiliation at the losing end of a linguistic dual now that peer pressure is more important in social relationships.

Creative rather than memorized comebacks become increasingly important during junior high and high school, and even into adulthood. The content of ritualized insults in junior high and high school reflects mature concerns about sexuality, origin, self-worth and group identity.

In our modern age of television, many comebacks and putdowns are learned from watching situation comedies. Sitcoms are full of one-liners, insults and putdowns that often find their way into schools the next day. This is not to blame television as the culprit, however. T.V. sitcoms merely reflect the society in which we live. Ours is a culture that teaches polite behavior, but which also loves a good, well-placed insult when the time is right.

During adolescence, opponents of ritual insult matches must verbally outsmart their rivals. This is usually done is a social situation. After all, what good is a great insult if there's no one there to hear it? Typically, rivals accuse each other of being homosexuals or offspring of incest, put down the father's job, or make accusations about the mother's promiscuity or sexuality. Sample ritual insults:

- **What's it like to have parents who were sister and brother?**
- **Is your dad still riding shotgun for the garbage company?**

Ritual insults are often culturally oriented. Cross-cultural insults make fun of stereotypes or insult the rival's beliefs. Young Hispanics, for example, insult each other's mothers because mothers are a highly emotive symbol of the hispanic culture. Some Hispanics fight at the mere mention of the words, *"your mother,"* without any specific insult stated. The implication is that "your mother is a prostitute."

The humor of ritual insults is hostile and aggressive. Like pranks, insults, putdowns, and comebacks are only funny to the winner. Victims of insults find no humor in humiliation. In a group situation, individuals are delighted when group members outsmart the competition. Insult matches are repeated and embellished in retellings throughout the day.

Not all insults are meant to be hostile. *"False insults"* are playful ways to call attention to friends even though we are calling them *"ugly"* or *"stupid."* This kind of false insulting during adolescence is often a form of flirting, just as hitting someone with a lunchbox can be a mating call for elementary school students. Laughing at someone's joking insults is a positive response to flirting behavior.

Racism and Sexism in Jokes

Laughing at others makes us feel superior. It also makes people feel better about things they are afraid of like ignorance, ugliness or weakness. Feeling superior (and fearful) is what ethnic, gender and religious jokes are all about.

Unfortunately, students often learn racist and sexist jokes at home. Students (and parents) may be completely unaware that their jokes contain messages that may be offensive to others because prejudices and values have been learned culturally from one generation to the next. Education is clearly the solution to inappropriate joking that occurs out of ignorance and hate.

Ethnic, religious and gender jokes are based on stereotypes, usually out of ignorance of someone else's culture or gender. One way to deflate the humor of ethnic, religious or gender jokes is to educate students about human similarities and differences.

Exercise: *Choose one ethnic group per month and discuss their stereotypes. Present ethnic jokes for each ethnic group and discuss how the stereotype is incorrect. Have students do reports to prove how stereotypes are false. For example: Have students do reports on hardworking Mexicans to show how Mexicans are not lazy. Explain that the lazy stereotype comes from a cultural difference ... that Mexicans take a nap in the afternoon because the weather is hot and not because they are lazy.*

Pranks

Pranks are one-sided humorous events, often associated with learning situations. People who devise pranks are seeking power over a victim, although pranksters are often unaware of the motivation behind what they do. Pranksters rarely empathize with their victims, which is why pranks are especially hostile and cruel.

Pranks usually begin around the time children start school. Elementary school children devise pranks or practical jokes against other children, family members, or teachers.

The purpose of most pranks is to embarrass the victim. Age-old classroom pranks include noise-making (farts are still a favorite), pigtail pulling, lifting a girl's dress up to expose underwear, sticking gum in books or placing fake vomit on the teacher's desk. The fun for pranksters is to see their classmates "get in trouble" while they remain anonymous.

Many practical jokes or pranks are viewed as simple mischievous tricks. Television shows like "Candid Camera," "T.V.'s Bloopers and Practical Jokes" and "Totally Hidden Videos" teach children that adults have a positive attitude about practical jokes in our society. Having a sense of humor about the inconveniences of these jokes is considered to be a sign of a healthy sense of humor.

Pranks that prey on the innocence of new students or substitute teachers can be a kind of initiation rite. In some prep schools ingenious pranks are even traditional, sometimes becoming part of school legends. In early American schools, when students were called with the ringing of churchbells, a typical prank incapacitated the ringers so teachers had no way to summon their students.

Pranks are part of the initiation rites for new members of private clubs. Hopeful initiates willingly participate in self-deprecating activities in order to become accepted members of the group. Sorority and fraternity initiates are sometimes victims of dangerous pranks or "hazing." Every year hazing incidents on North American campuses lead to the severe injury or death of students.

While elementary school children are too young to learn about adult pranks, they are not too young to understand why dangerous pranks are bad. If more university students had learned about the potential danger of pranks as youngsters, perhaps more of them would understand how to empathize with victims and how to refuse dangerous prank assignments.

Teaching students about pranks is important because some pranks are dangerous. Every year, pranksters hurt classmates by pulling seats out from under them. Bomb threats to schools are costly and disruptive. Setting off the school fire alarm takes fire fighters away from real fires.

Laughter, Stupidity and Sin

Even into the twentieth century, discipline-conscious headmasters and mistresses considered classroom laughter to be both foolish and sinful. North American education systems inherited Church attitudes that frowned upon laughter in the classroom, associating it with sinfulness.

The association between laughter and sin can be traced at least as far back as the Bible, especially as it was interpreted by the Church Fathers. People like John Chrysostom (c. 345–407 A.D.) wrote that "laughter does not seem to be a sin, but it leads to sin." Other religious writers argued that the Bible never mentions saints, prophets, apostles or even God laughing, so it must be sinful. In fact, most Biblical references to laugh-ter have something to do with foolish disobedience and disrespect of authority.

Ironically, while fools are supposed to be imbeciles and idiots, i.e., stupid, many slang expressions insulting fools refer to their wisdom. Thus do we call clowns wise guys, wise crackers, wisenheimers and wiseacres.

Fools have also had a long association with jackasses, an animal (like the chicken) not noted for intelligence. Donkey ears were associated with stupidity in ancient Rome in the myth of greedy King Midas. In addi-tion to his foolish choice of a golden touch over more important things, Midas thought the music of Pan's pipe sounded better than Apollo's lyre. This upset Apollo so much that he gave King Midas a set of donkey ears. Yet, while fools are believed to be as stupid as donkeys, we also recognize that jokers say wise things. Thus we refer to clowns as wise asses and smart asses.

Another example of a term that mixes the stupidity and wisdom of the fool is "geek." In modern times we use this word to refer to a brainy individual, yet the original geek was a fool whose circus act included biting the head off a chicken.

III. THE ROLE OF THE CLASS CLOWN

The important social function of the clown is to see things in a humorous light, even things we are not supposed to laugh at. Clowns and fools, jesters, comedians and buffoons have always expressed the deepest fears of a group, helping individuals release anxiety and tension.

Virtually every group has its clown. Still, it's difficult to imagine the great philosophers of ancient Rome and Greece being playful in the classroom, but they were. Plato was very much the class clown, some-times making fun of the bald spot on his teacher's (Socrates) head.

When the Gregorian calendar replaced the Roman Calendar of Julius Caesar in 1582, some were slow to follow the new system. Instead of celebrating the new New Year on January first as the Gregorian calendar did, many celebrated New Year's according to the old calendar, on April first. We still celebrate April Fools' Day on the first of April, a tribute to the fool in society. In the words of Mark Twain, *"Let's be thankful for the fools. If it weren't for them, the rest of us could not succeed."*

Whatever attitudes might have existed about clowns in the past, we now recognize clowning in the classroom as a sometimes positive expression. When clowning is witty and not terribly disruptive, it is considered to be a form of creativity. Clowning that takes the form of horseplaying is sometimes a way slow students get attention and approval they cannot muster with high grades.

Hostile clowns are students who may be calling for help, or they may be budding cynics who offer alternative views. The primary function of the class clown, however, remains that of social commentator since clowns often express thoughts that other students are afraid to verbalize.

Games Students Play

No parent wants to believe that their "little lumkins" is disruptive, unruly or downright rude. Some parents will say the child is just HYPERACTIVE. But attributing all class clown misbehavior to hyperkinesis is like saying all fat people have a gland problem.

The nightmarish truth is that there isn't just one clown out there. Every student is a potential class clown, armed to the teeth with paper airplanes and spitballs that will take flight at the first sign of weakness or opportunity.

No teacher wants to deal with a room full of uncooperative, sometimes hostile students. But the fact is, students will play games. It is their job to challenge you, and our job to deal with them fairly, no matter what they do. Here are a few games you may recognize:

Name Games: Who's On First?

One of the most common types of student games tests your ability to remember 500 names in a few seconds. Even with memory games, you can't do it and they know it. Name games can easily turn into a *"Who's On First"* routine, especially on the first day of school, especially for new teachers and substitutes.

A variation of the Name Game requires twins or similar looking students to confuse the teacher by changing seats, or by changing names in midday, just when you thought you had it right.

To avoid name games, have students keep name tags on desks or pinned to shirts and blouses.

Interruption

Another typical student game is *Interruption*. Points accrue for bubble-popping, knuckle-cracking, paper-crunching, fake coughing attacks and tongue clicking. Students also score if they are pen-clickers, wigglers, note-passers, whistlers, hand-wavers and Hawaiian love-callers.

Interruption has an upwardly mobile momentum. You can expect that once someone is successful at avoiding discipline by disrupting the lesson, others will follow suit because there is social pressure to go with the crowd. The ultimate goal of interruption is to get you to explode. There's nothing quite as fun as seeing someone who is normally reserved blowing their cool.

Make sure you don't fall victim to the purpose of the disruptive clown's game by staying in control without losing your temper. This doesn't mean keeping your suffering to yourself like a medieval martyr. Neither should you have to beg for reasonable behavior, even when groveling works.

The goal of every class clown is to get attention, from you and other students. Some clowns will react favorably to receiving special attention. Others don't want to play the teacher's pet, and these students will take advantage of your attempts to modify their behavior by giving them more responsibility.

Part of the solution to this game is to realize that disruptions usually carry secondary meanings that have nothing to do with the disruptions themselves. Students may be telling you they are bored or angry about some perceived unfairness. When the game of Interruption begins, stop what you are doing and communicate. Ask students what is wrong, and if they seem unable to express themselves, help them along. Reason with them, allowing them to express their thoughts and feelings too.

Oh, really?!

Oh, really?! is a game in which students pretend they are sincerely interested in the anecdote about your trip to Fiji a hundred years ago. The purpose of this game is to change the subject so students can relax their minds and play instead of going back to work. If students sense a lull in your mood, Oh, really?! requires them to ask more questions until you realize you've been duped. Anyway, it was fun reminiscing, wasn't it?

I'm Innocent!

Disruptive clowns play this game by pretending they don't have any idea what you're talking about, knowing perfectly well that it is statistically impossible to drop a pencil as often as thirty times in one class period. This kind of game has a cumulative effect on the psyche of both students and teachers; a building up of tensions until the number two pencil breaks the camel's back, so to speak.

Who Me?, like other disruptive games, often carries secondary meanings. The class clown may be trying to get your attention so you won't call on him/her and discover they are unprepared. In other cases, the class clown is speaking for the rest of the group, looking for a diversion because they are bored or because they hope to postpone something unpleasant, like a test.

Again, communicate with your students when they pretend to be stupid. Remain calm, be adult, and logical. Then go home and kick your cat.

You Said!

"You Said!" is a game students play when they pretend to believe you broke a rule or promise. Students rely on routine to know when and how to do the right thing. We adults, with our short-term memories often distracted, can forget promises, oathes or directions we gave last summer during summer school, but students do not. Pity the poor substitute who is told at every turn, *"That's not the way Mrs. Smith does it!"*

Students use rule games to postpone real work. When students protest a change in routine, explain to them that change is sometimes a good thing, and so is flexibility. You can empathize with students by saying something like, *"I realize it can be frustrating to be surprised, but in life you will encounter many surprises."* This is effective whether students are playing a prank on a substitute, or holding you to an ancient promise.

At the same time, *You Said* may be a form of protest that expresses perceived unfairness that can lead to more disruptive games (like *Interruption*). In this case, be flexible with students and open the negotiation table.

How Should I Know?

Hostile class clowns use sarcasm to get a laugh. One way hostile students do this is to answer your questions with a sarcastic question like *"How Should I Know."* Example:

Does anyone know what time it is?
—What, do I look like a watch?

Hostile class clowns use sarcasm to avoid attention, usually about their ability to perform or compete in the classroom. By making a joke when they answer a question, they divert our attention from the fact that they are unprepared or unable to grasp the lesson.

The best way to stop this game is to confront issues like homework, study skills and test taking in private, tutoring the slow student so they are better able to give right answers.

No One Here But Us Chickens

You have just walked into your classroom at the beginning of the day or class period. Nothing is wrong, except you sense something isn't quite right. Instinctually, you realize everyone knows something but you, but when you ask your students what it's about, they'll tell you, *"there's no one here but us chickens."* Begin to worry if there are tacks on your seat, rubber vomit on your desk or that something's about to jump at you from an unopened drawer.

In the event a prank is the effort of an entire class of clowns, there is always the possibility that a snitch will fill you in on what occurred in your absence. However, rules of class clown behavior are against confiding in the enemy, particularly when everyone is involved in the prank.

The main way students can organize sufficiently to play *No One Here But Us Chickens* is to give them time to do so. This is one game students play as a form of protest when teachers arrive late to class. Remember that students demand our total attention, and then some. Arrive early to greet them, smile and show you care and they are less likely to play pranks like this one.

IV. DISCIPLINING THE CLASS CLOWN

Early school room sketches show teachers disciplining class clowns by forcing them to sit in the corner wearing dunce caps, a practice that came from the earliest schools.

The dunce cap originated in Medieval Europe during a religious controversy led by John Duns Scotus (c. 1266–1308). The followers of Duns Scotus wore the triangular hats we now recognize as the dunce cap. Rival religious groups thought the dunces were fools.

Medieval teachers often decorated dunce caps with donkey ears since the jackass was associated with stupidity. In the early decades of this century, class clowns were still being forced to wear donkey ears or sit on a makeshift donkeys made in the same shape as "horses" used in modern roadblocks.

In today's humane world, we no longer consider humiliation as an effective disciplinary tactic. Peer pressure places restrictions on some class clowning. But what can we do when class clowning moves from mildly amusing to extremely unfunny?

Be Brief, But Firm

In most cases, ignoring simple disruptions, or confronting them with abbreviated discipline (Enough!), will allow you to return to the lesson as quickly as possible.

Most students don't want to get in trouble with teachers or parents, and a certain amount of fear is instilled with abrupt but stern commands. In part, this is based on a fear of the unknown. Most students won't want to test you once you verbalize a rule.

But what if the clowning disruptions resume?

The best way to deal with disruptive clowning is to create a classroom environment that does not encourage disruptive behavior born of boredom. The problem is that class clowns may be students who are bored in ANY environment. Class clowns want to have fun and to be the ones to initiate the good time, often at everyone else's expense. Still, there are a few tips that might help to control class clowning in most situations:

Do's

Do be flexible about group rules against individual needs.
Do be sensitive to changes in class mood. Establish a rapport with your students.
Do gear lessons to several intellectual levels.
Do smile and show enthusiasm. Let students know you like them and your job.
Do be courteous and respectful of students.
Do be consistent and fair.
Do encourage students often.
Do make sure students understand classroom laws.
Do allow students to opinionate about the logic and fairness of class rules.
Do be open to negotiation.
Do come to school well rested and with interesting lesson plans.
Do be natural, flexible, honest, positive and straightforward.

Don'ts

Don't forget your role as teacher and adult. Don't try to be "pals" with your students.
Don't use double standards of punishment based on sex, race or religion.
Don't ridicule.
Don't punish excessively.
Don't punish publicly when humiliation will cause greater conflict.

V. GROUP LAUGHTER

For most students, school is the most structured experience of their young lives. Joining a group in the classroom and having to share the attention of the teacher, is psychologically uncomfortable compared to the preschool years of freedom and personal attention from mommy. In part, schoolroom pranks are a protest against this more restrictive environment with its greater demands for order, obedience and conformity.

Laughter in a group depends on the social context of the humorous event. Each class creates its own unique sense of humor, distinct from the sense of humor that exists among individual members of the group—but also a product of the collective sense of humor. While one group of students may be gregarious and responsive to jokes, another will be bored or hostile.

School group members feel like they are part of a family with things in common like the teacher, their ages, subject matter covered, similar daily experiences at home and at school. There are also shared friendships, shared meals, and shared challenges or defeats.

While student groups feel like they are part of a family, the classroom is also a highly competitive place. Individual students compare themselves to other group members, deciding how they measure up in terms of intelligence, age, gender, race, religion, economic class, education level, experiential background and physical features and abilities.

The classroom is a place where individual students conform to group rules in order to pursue common educational goals. Discipline requires conformity at a time when individual students are still discovering their own unique identities. Some students will feel frustrated when the needs of the group come first.

Most students are willing to conform to classroom protocol in order to avoid potentially painful confrontations with adults.

In order to appreciate the group dynamics of laughter in the classroom, it must always be remembered that most classrooms are headed by adults who wield totalitarian power. The presence of the teacher and his or her ability to grant praise and good grades, as well as criticism and parental wrath, are never completely forgotten by student group members.

In the somewhat restrictive environment of the classroom, students are aware of rules and regulations of acceptable behavior. Students learn to speak when they are called upon, to follow the commands of the teacher, and to inhibit spontaneous behavior including laughter and physical movement. For this reason, most of the laughter that occurs in the classroom is characterized as *"suppressive laughter,"* a product of inhibition and naughtiness.

A group's sense of humor depends on many things including the social makeup of the group, the physical comfort and layout of the room, student interest in the subject matter, the attitude of the teacher and the time of day. One group may find a joke hilarious, while another may feel offended. Understand that it is not necessarily the quality or subject matter of the joke, but the social dynamics of the class itself that creates the humorous event.

Some of what we know about why some student groups laugh while others do not can be observed in a typical stand-up comedy club like *Dangerfield's* in New York or *The Improv* in Los Angeles. Professional comics realize that people feel more comfortable about laughing in a group than they do when sitting by themselves. Teachers, too, will find students are more enthusiastic when they are together than when they are allowed to spread themselves about in isolated groups throughout the room.

People also feel more comfortable about laughing among friends than they do among strangers. When a group of students has a good rapport with each other and the teacher, their camaraderie is likely to be expressed with a good sense of classroom humor. At the same time, students are more likely to laugh at "in jokes" among close friends than they are to laugh at jokes told by members outside their group of friends.

Group members who feel close also share the same sense of humor. Especially during adolescence, joking behavior may be used to invite members into a closed social group or to exclude non-members from socializing with them.

Group Glee

Elementary school children are decidedly uninhibited about expressing themselves in school-centered play activities. When a teacher announces recess or other good news, students react with uninhibited cheers, laughter and clapping. This phenomena is called "group glee." Group glee is contagious and more exciting because the group heightens the experience by generating extra enthusiasm among group members.

Group glee typifies student behavior during parties, holidays, recess and field trips, and any other time it is inconvenient for you. Acceptable levels of group glee is a healthy indication of class comaraderie. The underside of group glee is that individuals can feel less responsible for their behavior when in an emotional group. For this reason, teachers have to control delight and excitement so students don't endanger group safety or destroy property. In fact, students expect a certain amount of reasonable discipline. They just disagree about what "reasonable" means.

Gender and Groups

Throughout history, joking has been a male-dominated behavior. Both primitive and modern societies place taboos on female clowning behavior and the use of taboo language by women. Even in the relatively permissible society that exists in North America, there are far more professional male comics than females.

Males may develop a more assertive and expressive sense of humor because they are biologically more aggressive or because they are socialized to be less inhibited. Passivity in females may be both a product of biology (X and Y chromosomes) as well as learned behavior. Little girls are more restricted in their play, while boys are encouraged to be rough. Little boys are also more likely to escape punishment for aggressive behavior than girls.

Standards of modesty are more conservative for girls and girls have more restrictions placed on their language, dress and general behavior. Some studies show that girls are socialized to have a greater need for social approval than boys. At the same time, while girls are taught to be modest and passive, females usually develop better language skills as joke tellers.

Girls more often take a passive role as joke tellers, while boys are more active, telling cruder jokes and doing so more often. Fewer female students, for example, resort to poo-poo cushions and plastic vomit for a laugh.

Because females are socialized to a greater extent to be responsive to jokes, they are also more likely to laugh long and hard at a humorous event than boys. Boys are more often boisterous laughers, laughing loud and with horseplaying and roughhousing. In addition, boys are more likely to take part in aggressive forms of joking including pranks and practical jokes.

As students become socialized, they come to understand the behavior expected of their gender. Sex role stereotyping is related to play in the toys assigned to each gender. Students may protest participation in activities they believe is a threat to their gender identity. Boys, for example, may refuse to play with dolls or may not be permitted to do so by parents. Girls may be discouraged from playing with trucks or war toys, and parents may not permit them to participate in aggressive sports.

Joking is one way people resocialize individuals who deviate from sex roles. Hostile insults make fun by calling aggressive females "tomboys" and passive boys "queers" or "sissies." Some adult homosexuals admit that elementary school gibes about their sexuality were a painful and confusing part of their childhood.

Sexual typing in joking relationships begins with the first joke-telling experiences. All joking relationships allow specific levels of touching, horseplaying, insulting and the use of taboo words and subjects. It is less common for children to use obscenities or to horseplay with people of the opposite gender, but they may tell "dirty" jokes among members of the same sex.

Effective Seating Plans

The arrangement of desks in the classroom can affect the overall humorous mood of your student group. The optimal position of group members in the classroom depends on the unique chemistry of your students. Some disruptive laughing can be avoided by separating joking friends in class.

Traditional classrooms positioned desks so that all students faced the front of the room. Students may be less inclined to laugh when their behavior is being scrutinized by other students as when desks are placed in a horseshoe shape. Another class, seated in the same horseshoe, might laugh more than usual because they are in a position to see their peers laugh.

Students will laugh more when they are in a group than when they are alone. The larger the group, the more boisterous students can become as every assembly monitor or recess duty teacher already knows.

People also laugh more in low lights. Theater audiences, for example, will laugh freely and boisterously at jokes that individual members of the audience might find only mildly amusing. It is not surprising, then, that students laugh more freely when lights are low during films or assemblies.

Laughter, like yawning, is contagious. Students laugh louder and harder in a group because group sanctions allow more freedom to laugh at taboo subjects and to laugh without physical inhibitions. Sometimes students laugh as part of a group even though they don't think something is really funny, because they want to feel like part of the group. The shared experience of group laughter feels good as the sharing of emotions implies friendship and love. Laughing as a member of a group makes all of us feel we are socially accepted and that we are not alone in the world.

Chapter 4

THE TEACHER AS ENTERTAINER

*Give a boy a sense of humor and a sense of proportion and
he'll stand up to anything.*

Goodbye, Mr. Chips, James Hilton

I. ROLE MODEL VS. HUMAN BEING

The first teachers were parents who passed knowledge to their children about family and tribal history, survival skills and social protocol. Students acquired professional knowledge by working as apprentices for master craftsmen, often older family members.

As towns and cities grew, schools became more formalized. Teachers were learned people, often without families of their own, who ruled with dictatorial powers over their students. Since the beginning of organized education, teachers have been among the pillars of society, held up as the community's most important role models. With the exception of our political leaders, there is no other job in which individuals are held more accountable for their behavior than the teaching profession. This puts a lot of pressure on the human side of teachers, that side where the sense of humor is most likely to be found.

Students want a teacher who has a sense of humor, but not necessarily someone who stands in front of the class telling jokes like a stand-up comic. Nevertheless, teachers have much in common with professional entertainers. Like them, teachers must hold the interest of their "audience" while they "perform." Like professional entertainers, teachers eventually learn to deal effectively with unanticipated interruptions, malfunctioning equipment, and even an occasional "heckler" in the back of the room.

In many ways, the teacher's job is more demanding than that of the professional comic. In addition to entertaining, we must prove ourselves as miracle workers, super humans and all-things-to-all-people. In a way, teachers are miracle workers, breaking more laws of nature than any other profession. Among the things we disprove every day:

> Matter can neither be created nor destroyed.
> There are 60 minutes in an hour.
> If you do something long enough, you will get better at it.
> The most important thing is to try your best.
> Everything has its bright side.
> It can't get any worse.

If the roads of Hell are paved with good intentions, I'm sure there are some lesson plans down there somewhere. Every teacher soon learns you have to be flexible to cope with the unpredictable nature of the average school day. It is the adaptable teacher who is most likely to have fun teaching, fun that is contagious in the classroom. More importantly, your sense of humor is sometimes the only thing that will carry you through the rough times. This section is about developing a comic technique as a professional skill.

Developing a Comic Technique

Professional entertainers develop a comic technique by practicing over a long period of time. As a teacher, you are in a unique position to practice your act since you have a captive audience five days a week. Like the professional entertainer, you will sharpen your skills with experience. Here are a few tricks of the trade:

- **Discover what makes your students laugh.** *You can do this by watching their television programs and reading the humor books written for them. Listen to their jokes and discover what they think is funny, especially things that don't amuse most adults.*

- **Start a comedy file.** *Every time a joke "works" in your class, write it on an index card and file it away for future use. This is important because it is natural to forget our best jokes, especially when they are situational. Categories in your comedy file can include things like "rainy days" or "hot days" when humor can relieve stress in an uncomfortable room. You can also categorize jokes by subjects you cover every year in your class.*

- **Start a comedy library.** *Begin by collecting joke anthologies compiled for professional speakers and entertainers. Many of these anthologies will contain jokes that are not funny in written form but which may be adapted to your classroom under the right circumstances. Again, when you find something in your comedy library that tickles your funny bone, file it in your comedy file for easy access.*

- **Plan to interject jokes into your lessons.** *As you plan your lessons from one week to the next, see if there isn't some time when a funny anecdote can be included along with the math and reading. Experts tell us students like a change of pace every 15 minutes. Jokes and the laughter they cause are a great way to stretch the mind and body in between more serious lessons.*

- **Cultivate classroom jokes.** *In every group there are "in jokes" that make the group feel like part of a family. Your class "joke" can be an imaginary character who tells you funny things, a class pet, or a pet project. Class clowns can also bring students together with their jokes, although clowns do expect teachers to control joking behavior when it becomes inappropriate or disruptive.*

Teacher Stress

Even in a book on humor in the classroom it would be naive to suggest that all school days are fun days. Even on the best days, teaching can be a difficult and stressful job. Sometimes it's impossible to have a sense of humor when there are problem students, overcrowded classrooms, low salaries or limited budgets for supplies. This is not to mention insensitive administrators, parents who side with their kids no matter what students do, and professional jealousy in the workplace.

Many jokes about education make light of the frustration caused by poor students as in the following examples:

Poor study habits:

> What are the three most common words students use?
> I don't know.

> What's the difference between a poor student and a clock?
> Time passes.

Cheating:

> Mr. Jones distributed corrected tests. "Sandy," he said to a student known for cheating, "You weren't far from passing."
> "I know," said Sandy. Just two seats.

> Mrs. Smith approached little Johnny in class one day. "I read that report you wrote on the family dog," she said. "It was just like the report your brother wrote for me last week, word-for-word."
> "Same dog," Johnny quipped.

Disciplinary Problems:

> The students were returning from a field trip when they spotted the bus driver. They raced to greet him, asking questions in chattering voices. At first the driver was amused, but then some students got in a fight and some others kicked his bus. A few minutes passed when the teacher appeared, hair disheveled and face drawn.
> "Are these your students, or is this a picnic!" snapped the bus driver.
> "These are my students," replied the teacher, "and this is no picnic."

Part of the stress of teaching has nothing to do with students and the joys of the classroom, but with the other teachers. Stress among colleagues comes from personality conflicts as well as the way different people perceive their jobs.

Personality conflicts are inevitable if you work with someone who is condescending, overbearing, jealous or a gossip. But these kind of personalities exist in every work place. At least as a teacher, you have the autonomy of your classroom, something which attracts many individuals to the profession. Most teachers go into teaching because they see themselves as professionals. But some only end up as teachers by accident. These people feel like they're in a rut, that life is unfair, or that their job is boring because they are underchallenged.

It is well known that the stress of teaching is a cumulative one. Like the "seven-year itch" in marriage, teachers may need to take a sabbatical after many years of teaching to feel rejuvenated. If you wake up one day and realize you haven't laughed in years, you may want to consider taking a brief break, or changing jobs altogether.

When you are feeling blue temporarily, there's nothing like a break in the routine to get you back in the mood. Here are a few rut breakers that may help:

Redecorate your room; move the furniture, change the decor.

Take a break from lectures with a fun movie.

Plan a trip or class project.

Invite a guest speaker to teach your class for a day.

Enlist a fun parent as a classroom assistant.

Switch rooms; if weather permits, take the class outside. If a room is available, teach in another room, like the auditorium.

Give yourself a make over; new hairstyle, new clothes.

Start a fun club that allows you to spend more time with a favorite hobby.

Treat yourself to dinner or lunch (no dieting).

Redo your house, listening to upbeat music.

Go on an exciting trip, go abroad or someplace really different.

Compile a reading list of fun books, and read them at leisure.

Organize a support group and share feelings with friends.

Plan a fun party of peers (come-as-you-are or come-as-you-wish-you-were costume parties are always fun).

II. JOKING RELATIONSHIPS

Much of what we know about the group dynamics of laughter comes from the study of anthropology. Anthropologists have isolated predictable "joking relationships" that exist between friends, family members, and strangers of different ages and gender.

Among the anthropologists who studied joking relationships was A. R. Radcliffe-Brown. According to Radcliffe-Brown, the purpose of joking in any society is to pacify hostility between family and non-family members.

Joking relationships are subject to social sanctions around the context of a situation, roles, age and gender. Joking also depends on the social hierarchy of group members and expectations about the outcome of the joking communication.

Joking relationships between equal peers are easily formed and have few restrictions. Among equal peers joking can include friendly or hostile teasing. The greater the differences among group members, the more restrictions exist between jokers.

People of unequal status experience a different kind of joking relationship than equal peers. Parent-child, teacher-student, and boss-employee joking have greater restrictions on joke content and joke initiation as well as taboos on the appropriate time and place for joking.

People of lesser status feel some intimidation or awe when a more important or powerful person tells a joke. People of lesser status are more responsive to powerful jokesters, laughing at their jokes out of respect and fear. In addition, powerful people are more likely to initiate joking and to do so more often, in part, because they have less fear of reprisals for making light of issues.

The more powerful a person is perceived, the less they are viewed as having a sense of humor. Popes, presidents and principals are stereotypically serious, even if they smile and laugh a lot in reality. Few portraits of powerful people show them smiling or laughing because happiness is associated with weakness and stupidity.

Not only is it taboo to joke with the highest powers in many societies, it is also a sign of disrespect to make fun of powerful people. The restrictions on joking relationships with powerful beings makes it tempting to paint mustaches on portraits of powerful people, or to caricature teachers on chalkboards. Taboos against joking about powerful beings includes godheads. While Jesus Christ may appear as a character in golf jokes, it will offend many people if he is ridiculed.

The Child-Parent Joking Relationship

Meeting parents is a good way to understand your student's sense of humor, or lack of it. This is important because a student's joking relationship with role models at home will probably be transferred to the adult teacher in school.

Joking with mom or dad usually depends on the disposition of the parents. Serious moms and dads are less likely to cultivate joking relationships with their children than parents with an active, expressive sense of humor.

Parents teach youngsters when it is acceptable to initiate joking behavior. Joking in front of visitors as an attention grabber may be encouraged or discouraged. Parents usually discourage joking during church, at funerals, or when they are busy working at home. Parents who send laughing children away too often will discourage youngsters from attempting to achieve goals in this way. This may influence a child's reluctance to be playful with teachers at school as well.

Parents exercise the greatest influence over the preschooler's sense of humor. Among other things, parents will teach their youngsters to respect or disrespect adult authority. Children need to be able to laugh at all-powerful adults who control every aspect of their lives, but should be taught to do so in a socially acceptable way. It is permitted, for example, to laugh at clowns or adults who are trying to be silly. It is impolite to laugh at deformity, racial differences or human suffering.

One way to better understand the parent's perspective is to examine jokes about parents and their school-age children. Jokes from the child's perspective make fun of double standards that exist between little people and adults who say things like, *"Do as I say, not as I do."* Here's one joke to illustrate this disparity:

> The teacher asked Suzie, "Why do you have that string tied around your finger?"
> Suzie said, "Mommy didn't want me to forget to mail her letter."
> "Did you mail it?"
> "I couldn't. Mommy forgot to give it to me."

Parent-child jokes often express anxiety parents feel about how smart their kids are in school. Parents don't want to appear ignorant as kids learn new math, computer skills, foreign languages or other subjects which parents might not feel comfortable about themselves. For example, there was the mother who bragged that her daughter was taking Spanish and geometry. *"Go ahead,"* she said when her daughter entered the room. *"Speak to me in geometry."* Here's are two other jokes that make light of the fear of new knowledge:

> Father: Son, it's time we had a talk about sex.
> Son: Sure, what'ya wanna know?

> Johnny came home from school one day and mother asked him what he learned.
> "We learned how to count," Johnny beamed.
> "Very good," said Mother. "How much is 2 + 2?"
> "Seven," Johnny answered.
> "Hey, that kid's pretty smart," his father replied. "He only missed it by one."

Another set of jokes reveals worries parents have about their kids getting in trouble at school:

> Freddie came home and asked his father, "Do you think people should be punished for something they didn't do?"
> "Of course not," his father said.
> "Good," said Johnny. "Because I didn't do my homework."

Jokes about school from the student's perspective express fears about school frustrations, as in the following example:

> Patti came home from school on the first day, looking sad and glum.
> "Did you get home sick today," her mother asked.
> "No," said Patti. "I got school sick."

Then there was the student who came home and complained, *"I can't read and I can't write, and now the teacher says I can't talk!"*

The Student-Teacher Joking Relationship

A child's attitude towards teachers is often a reflection of how parents feel about educators. Parents who had bad experiences in school may pass negative feelings to children, either consciously or unwittingly.

If parents have done a good job socializing their children, students will already have a sense of what is appropriate joking behavior in school. In each class, students will learn how individual teachers feel about when it is acceptable to laugh at school, and when laughter will get them into trouble.

First-graders learned at home how smiles, laughter and crying effectively achieved their adult-centered goals. The emotional tactics (laughing or crying) that worked during the first five or six years at home are inclined to be repeated when students try to get what they want from teachers at school, usually praise, attention and good grades.

Most elementary school students love and respect adults and enjoy a good joking relationship with teachers. As students mature, however, they become more self-conscious, worrying about how others perceive them.

Peer pressure becomes increasingly important through junior high and high school. While there is much joking between in-group members throughout adolescence, most teenage students avoid joking relationships with adults.

Perceiving adults as unfunny typifies the generation gap between adolescents and "old people" like teachers and parents, who were born in the time of the dinosaurs. Not thinking adults are funny or that adults are out-of-touch with teenage fashion and music are simply part of the defiance and independence that marks young adulthood.

Since a joking relationship characterizes mutual understanding and shared concerns, the greater the age difference between adolescents and adults, the wider the communication rift can be, and the less likely mutual moments are shared in the form of laughter. Ultimately, adolescents develop an adult sense of humor as they begin to experience adult concerns associated with careers, finances and mature relationships.

The Parent-Teacher Joking Relationship

The relationship between teachers and parents can be strained or pleasant. Smiles from teachers communicate friendliness and relieve anxiety parents may feel about talking to their children's teacher. Smiles also open the doors to communication about mutual concerns.

Laughter between parents and teachers, however, is often another subject. Parents may perceive laughter as joking, even when it is not intended as such. Few parents will find amusement in jokes about their child, no matter how silly the joke might be. Many parents see jokes as attacks against them. This protective instinct in parents disallows any joke that might indicate you do not take a student seriously. The protective parental attitude causes some parents to take their children's side no matter what, as the following joke reveals:

> **"Who knocked down the Walls of Jerico," the teacher asked.**
> **"It wasn't me," said Johnny.**
> **The teacher invited Johnny's mother for a meeting. "I think Johnny has a problem," the teacher said. "I asked him who knocked down the Walls of Jerico and he said he didn't do it."**
> **"Look," said Johnny's mother. "If my son said he didn't knock down that wall, he didn't do it."**
> **In desperation, the teacher called in Johnny's father. "Your son needs help," said the teacher. "I asked him who knocked down the Walls of Jerico and he said he didn't do it."**
> **"All right," said the father. "How much is this wall going to cost me."**

There is a certain "otherness" that exists between parents and teachers when it comes to the education of their children. Parents trust teachers to educate their children, but worry that teachers won't be as attentive as they should. Parents hope teachers will not set poor examples, teach bad lessons, or dislike their children.

Parents also fear teachers both as symbols of authority and as the people in charge of their children's success. Many parents would rather believe a teacher is inadequate than admit their child is not perfect. At the same time, some jokes note the anxiety parents feel about their children getting in trouble at school:

> Johnny came home from school one day. Mother asked, "Why are you home so early?"
> "I was the first one to answer the question right," said Johnny.
> "What was the question?"
> "Who threw the paper airplane at Miss Jones."

The best way to communicate with parents is to do so directly. Teachers like to speak to parents in euphemisms because parents are so sensitive about their kids. However, to solve a behavior problem it is better to say things like *"Johnny keeps flushing paper towels down the toilet,"* rather than, *"Johnny misbehaves at school."* Specific behavior problems can be corrected better than vague ones which might give parents the impression you don't like the child.

The Student-Student Joking Relationship

Throughout the preschool years, young children are cute, inviting smiles and laughter from those around them. This early cuteness, and the laughter it causes, is confusing to toddlers because they are not trying to be funny intentionally. As children mature, however, they learn how to be cute and funny. By the time children enter school, they have learned to control their behavior to elicit the humorous response from others.

Your student's sense of humor in class is influenced, to a large extent, by their early social experiences with preschool play. Social experiences with humor begin around the age of two or three, when children start to share humor with others. Before that time, babies and toddlers spent most of their joyful times smiling or laughing to themselves when satiated, at the attention they received from others, and as they played and made-believe while discovering the world around them.

Preschoolers experiment with joke telling as they improve their general communication skills. As new joke tellers, children discover what makes others laugh and what does not. If they are effective joke tellers, they will probably repeat the behavior. If others do not think they are funny, they are less prone to continue attempts at humor.

All children learn that some kinds of laughter doesn't feel good, like when they are victims of hostile laughter. Whether students experience the laughter of scorn in the classroom or on the playground, it never feels good to be rejected by laughing classmates.

Admittedly, some students are more sensitive about being laughed at than others. Class clowns invite deprecating laughter and the attention it brings. Shy students can cry at the least hint of laughter by others, even when it is meant as a term of endearment, as in the case of false insults. In some cases, students misinterpret laughter, believing others are laughing at them even when it is untrue. Since students are not always sensitive to the nuances of inner feelings, teachers can explain why it is impolite or cruel when students laugh at each other in class.

The Teacher-Teacher Joking Relationship

Joking relationships between equal peers in the easiest to cultivate since many in-jokes come naturally to people who share similar experiences. It's important to develop joking relationships with fellow teachers. There is no better support network than one with people who truly understand the rigors of the job as well as the joys. At the same time, teaching is a business that requires human beings to interact with other human beings. This means dealing with some not-so-funny personalities as well as a certain amount of professional jealousy.

Professional jealousy is about as funny as a rock. There's nothing worse than a bitter fellow teacher who feels like life has passed them by. Sometimes professional jealousy is gender based, as when a man can't accept that a woman makes more money, teaches better courses or gets the promotion he felt he deserved. Other jealousy is racist, as when a black or white resents someone else's advancement, believing it is based more on skin color than merit. Some people are jealous because they are competitive and cannot accept anyone who makes more money, gets more education or more attention than they do. Jealousy is a fact of life, but it doesn't make the work environment of school any easier.

One way to cope with professional jealousy is to get the problem out in the open. Perhaps the jealousy is disguised as hostile "jokes," allowing the jealous person to deny their true feelings by saying they were "just kidding." Jealousy is one of those negative emotions that does nothing but make everyone miserable. In many cases, you need to confront the jealous person directly or it can get worse.

Jealous teachers are threatened by your talent and skills. Talking with them is one way to help them overcome feelings about their perceived lack of talent as a teacher. In most cases, talking with others about personal feelings will lead to the kind of closeness that allows a joking relationship, a sign of acceptance.

Not every jealous person wants to make friends with people they see as rivals. It may help to bring in a mediator. Your school counselor or psychologist may be better qualified to do this than a principal or headmaster, since counselors are specifically trained to understand the subtleties of personality conflicts and human nature.

Some people will never get along. You may have a healthy sense of humor while someone else does not. If you have done all you can to help a fellow teacher overcome a negative attitude to no avail, don't let the sourpuss drag you into their negative world.

There are many ways to inject humor and laughter into the typical school day, even when you are the only laughing teacher in a sea of humorless bores. One thing you can do is to begin every faculty meeting with a joke. I don't mean a bellylaughing wisecrack, but certainly something witty and ironic that fellow teachers can think about throughout the week. Mark Twain, Will Rogers and Daniel Webster are great sources of humorous quotes, many of them relevant to education.

Another way to begin a faculty meeting is to photocopy a comic strip that makes light of education. Peanuts, Funky Winkerbean, the Far Side and Pogo all feature schoolroom situations all teachers experience. Your newspaper may have a local artist who writes jokes about the classroom as well.

The Teacher-Administrator Joking Relationship

It is the relationship between teachers and administrators that is least often viewed as fun. Humorless conflicts that lead to teacher walkouts and strikes periodically occur between unhappy teachers and inflexible school board administrators. "Just remember," goes the joke, "there are always two sides to every argument, unless the principal is involved, in which case there is only one."

Jokes about administrators make fun of them for lacking a sense of humor and for being know-it-alls. For example:

> Mr. Jones, the principal at the Dade School, got lost in a residential neighborhood.
> As he passed a house, he recognized one of the students from his class.
> "Can you tell me how to get to Main Street?," he asked. "I seem to have lost my
> way." "I don't know how to get to Main Street," Johnny said.
> "Well, just tell me which way is downtown," the principal insisted. "I can find my
> way from there."
> "I don't know which way downtown is," said Johnny.
> "You don't know much of anything, do you," the principal snapped.
> "Maybe not," said Johnny, "But I'm not the one who's lost."

What do you do about an administrator who is a power-monger, especially one without a sense of humor? You might try looking on the positive side. After all, it could be worse. You could have an oppressive administrator who HAS a sense of humor, but uses it in a negative, condescending way.

The joking relationship between teacher and administrator is similar to the one that exists between parents and their children and between teachers and their students. As one youngster said overhearing her sister laugh, *"Suzie must be in trouble. She's laughing at dad's jokes."* Similarly, in the teacher-administrator joking relationship, administrators are more likely to initiate jokes while teachers are more inclined to respond favorably to the joke, especially if it could get you a raise. . . .

In fairness to principals and other administrators, it should be noted that they have a difficult job. It is their lot to cope with budgets, disciplinary problems and the needs of teachers, parents and community leaders. Here's a joke that sympathizes with the administrator's plight:

> Mrs. Smith told Johnny, "Get up. It's time to go to school."
> "I don't want to go to school," Johnny said.
> "You're forty years old and you're the principal, and you're going to school
> whether you like it or not," said Mrs. Smith.

Chapter 5

TEACHING CREATIVITY

Joy is but the sign that creative emotion is fulfilling its purpose.

Charles du Bos

The arts and crafts class offers a unique opportunity to cultivate your students' sense of humor creatively. Many traditional craft projects can be enlivened by varying the assignment in a humorous way. This chapter is about using creative projects to help students appreciate the lighter side of reality.

I. HUMOR AND CREATIVITY

There's a lot of speculation about what exactly creativity really is. Most agree that creative people have a heightened sensitivity which allows them to produce artwork and music. Psychologists note that creative people are usually impulsive, independent, introverted, intuitive and self-accepting.

Some psychologists believe that the cognitive processes involved in creating humor are similar to the processes that occur in other creative

58

insights. Creative children are more playful, are more likely to have imaginary playmates, and generally spend more time amusing themselves with daydreams.

Creative children initiate humor more frequently, understand humor better, and create more humorous material when they invent jokes. Creative people also appreciate a good sense of humor in classmates and friends.

Creativity is difficult to evaluate with standardized tests and traditional grading systems, especially when it takes the form of wittiness in joke telling. Like other unorthodox measures of intelligence, humor is not always recognized as an indication of aptitude. This is true not only because the genius of wit is difficult to calculate, but also because wittiness is too often expressed in socially disruptive ways. Nevertheless, wit may not only be an expression of creative aptitude, it may also be an indication of giftedness. Witty remarks reveal an ability to make unusual associations and to play with language in a more complex way.

The wonderful thing about youth is its innovative spirit. The ability and desire to try new things comes, in part, from the lack of inhibitions about the way things are SUPPOSED to be done. Students are ready to try new things adults have never considered before because many youthful ideas begin from a "tabula rasa," or "clean slate."

Inspiration

Young, creative minds often express themselves in their artwork. Young students love to work with their hands, but they often need direction in choosing a subject for their masterpieces. There are many ways you can help your students express their sense of humor in their arts and crafts projects.

Creative activities are open-ended, allowing students to be spontaneous and creative above the parameters of the exercise. Teachers who encourage an inventive spirit permit students to try new things, from innovative science experiments to new ways of approaching the Three R's.

Students will test your willingness to let them be creative, constantly. The trick for every teacher, and the lesson for every student, is to decipher the difference between creativity and misbehavior; between spontaneity and rudeness.

The Joy of Accomplishment

Every fun lesson can be a creative learning experience in the craft class. Artwork is the perfect "hands-on" supplement to academic lessons. In craft class an element of play is added to school. It is a place where students can mess their hands, smear their fingers with paint and paste and turn to scissors to cut out the numbers, letters, words or creatures they have learned about in school.

Most playful school activities do not require big budget items or weeks of lesson planning. A few simple materials in combination with a student's imagination are all that is needed to carry out a playful learning exercise.

II. SUPPLIES

Supplies for projects that teach students about their sense of humor are the same supplies you use in any arts and crafts class. Clay, drawing materials (paints, magic markers, crayons, colored chalk, pencils and pens), shiny materials (glitter, colored gravel, shellac, nail polish), paper supplies (colored, construction, tracing), ribbon, string, and yarn, scissors, sponges, and sticking materials (glue, paste, tape) are standard equipment in any craft class.

In addition to standard supplies, the arts and crafts box is the perfect repository for every kind of "throwaway," from thread spools to magazines. Old mittens can be cut up for pieces of wool. Aluminum foil, cotton balls, fabric scraps, feathers, popcycle sticks, rubber bands, shells, and toothpicks are just some of the items that will find their way into your craft box. A letter to parents will bring in more "supplies" than you can use.

In addition to providing materials, the arts and crafts teacher must provide direction. A model of the finished product will show students the ultimate goal and give them an ideal towards which they can work. Encouraging words and smiles of praise are always in order, especially for students who do not work well with their hands.

Clay

Young students love to play with clay because gooey stuff feels good. Working with maleable materials like hardening or non-hardening clay, dough mixes or glazing compound teaches manual dexterity and encourages creativity. In addition, funny clay figures make great gifts to surprise mom and dad at holiday time.

Making creatures funny requires students to exaggerate the ideal. Animals, people, spaceships, tiny bowls or insects can be made funny by attaching extra large or extra small appendages. Funny creature projects can be displayed around a theme, like a zany zoo, a crazy circus or a weird village.

Bodies can be fashioned from leftover cardboard paper towel or toilet tissue tubes, or from paper lunch bags or socks stuffed with newspaper. Exaggeration is a key element in the creation of a humorous event. Students can make funny animals using colored construction paper which can be cut into giant ears, enormous feet, big red noses, extra tiny heads or fat bellies.

Students can also create funny images by pressing objects like bottle caps, shells or buttons into clay. Students can make clown faces or funny people, animals or creatures with unusual or exaggerated features. Toothpicks can be used with clay to create appendages or to draw lines or tiny holes. To create a shiny finish, paint the clay figures with clear nail polish.

Paper

Snowflakes

Every snowflake is unique, just like every student. Maybe that's why snowflakes are always a favorite creation. Snowflakes together on a sunny bulletin board reflect a happy mood.

To make the snowflake have students take a piece of white paper and trim the edges to make a circle. Fold the circle in half, three times. Cut designs around all edges of the paper. Encourage students to be creative in the cut of their shapes (usually various combinations of half circles, squares or triangles). At the same time, make sure the cuts are not too long or severe, or there won't be much of a snowflake left to see.

When the paper is unfolded, unique geometric designs create a snowflake. Smear the snowflakes with a bit of paste or glue and make them sparkle with silver, gold or colored glitter.

Pasting the snowflake to a blue background creates a sky with room for the student's name. When all the snowflakes are ready, spread them about the bulletin board to create a classroom blizzard.

Paper spirals

It's easy to create a paper spiral by cutting a round piece of paper (or a paper plate) in a circle from the outer edge to the center. Use colored paper, or have students draw colorful abstract designs that become unique when the spiral is created.

When every child creates a colored spiral, these can be hung on a tree on holidays. At Easter, spirals can decorate a tree along with Easter eggs. At Christmas, spirals can function as Christmas ornaments. At Halloween, spirals can decorate a scary tree, and on St. Valentines Day, spirals can decorate a tree along with decorated hearts.

Collages

The word collage comes from the French word for "paste." A collage is an artform consisting of bits of objects pasted together incongruously, which makes them perfect vehicles for teaching humor appreciation. A funny collage can be any pasted collection of related parts, such as a photo montage.

Perhaps there is no better way to express a class's sense of comaraderie than to create a personal collage that reflects the individuals who make up the group. Students can create a collage of self-portraits, of flower drawings, or of designs that relate to a class project, like a classroom ant farm or science experiment.

Fun collages can be named or labeled with construction paper letters. Label the bulletin board collage something like, "Let's Have Fun." Here are a few ideas for humorous collages:

- *A joke collage forces students to be creative rather than to memorize standard answers to common jokes. Joke collages consist of magazine pictures or drawings that illustrate the answer to a joke or riddle. For example, a knock-knock collage would reveal possible answers to the question, "Who's There?"*
- *Have students search for funny faces to create a collage of human expression. A variation on this theme is a smile collage in which happy smiles are pasted haphazardly to create a medley of merry mouths.*
- *Students can also make a collage of funny words. Words may be funny because the letters are fat or extra thin, or because the sound of the word is humorous. This exercise helps students think about what kinds of words sound silly to them (like goofy or pickle). A humorous synonym collage*

requires students to bring in any word that has to do with fun (clown, mirth, party, etc.)

III. HUMOR IN ARTS AND CRAFTS

Imitation is at the heart of all learning, but it is also an important part of learning about the sense of humor. By observing others we learn what makes people laugh and what makes them cry. We learn how to cause laughter in others by imitating the world we see around us. Arts and crafts teach students to imitate the world around them, sometimes in a humorous way.

Mirror Drawings

Mirror drawing, like joke telling, teaches students to observe and imitate. Have students bring in a funny picture from a magazine. Let students decide what is funny so they cultivate their own individual sense of humor.

Cut the picture in half and paste it on a piece of paper. Students then recreate the missing side of the picture with magic markers or crayons.

As a variation of this exercise, have student make a mirror drawing in which the second half of their picture is the opposite of the original version.

Comics and Cartoons

Of all the humorous art forms, comic strips are most likely to transcend all age and gender boundaries. Many of us read the same comics as adults that we enjoyed as children. In part this is because comic strip art is simple but effective, offering instant gratification whether it is purely visual or visual in combination with a linguistic element.

Comics are rarely studied in the formal classroom. Nevertheless, there is much to learn from the dissection of a humorous strip. To do this, have students bring in their favorite comic strips. Tell them to bring in the Sunday paper to take advantage of colored comics. In class, analyze these comics by observing who the characters are, what their names are, what they wear and what kind of personality they have.

Once students have a comic strip model to follow, it's time to create their own comic strips. Do this as a class project or break students into teams. Let them create their own humorous characters, drawing bubbles where comic captions can be added later.

Professional comic strip artists admit that one of the most difficult things about their job is creating new things for the same characters to say day after day. In fact, when you analyze your comic strips you will note that the characters rarely change. They inhabit limited spaces and wear the same clothing year after year.

Students need to think ahead about the dimensions of their comic strip. Their characters should have names, specific dispositions and personalities, and a place around which the comic strip theme revolves. Perhaps they can draw a strip about going someplace fun or about funny things that happen after school. All of this should be decided before anyone actually begins to draw the strip.

Caricatures

Humorous events are digressions from the ideal. This is a concept which students need to learn to appreciate that something is funny. Caricatures are exaggerated renditions of an ideal; a fictitious drawing which is, nevertheless, based in reality.

To draw a caricature, students should focus on the most outstanding feature of a figure, and highlight the qualities that stand out most. To illustrate this, show students a picture of a person who is caricatured in your local newspaper. Have them discover this person's outstanding features. Now show students a caricatured version of the person. Has the artist exaggerated all the qualities students noticed as unusual, extra large or small?

When students understand what a caricature is, have them draw one for themselves. If you don't mind, let students draw a caricature of you and discover how they perceive your outstanding features. Students can pair up and draw each other. You can also have students bring in a magazine photo and let them caricaturize it.

Use the bulletin board to display student caricatures, along with the original "ideal," so they can see how effectively other students have used exaggeration to make light of a reality.

Another way to teach students to appreciate the art of caricature is to invite a local artist to your classroom. Newspaper cartoonists are some-times willing to do this. University art students may also be willing to volunteer. Your cartoonist can demonstrate how he or she draws political cartoons, or draw caricatures of the students.

Clown Art

The design of a circus clown's face is so unique that professional clowns copyright their makeup design. Students can create a classroom circus by designing their own unique clowns. Make funny clown faces using red or blue yarn for hair, bottle caps for eyes and sponges for noses.

Clown art begins with a simple face drawing on a paper plate. Create a mustache, beard, sideburns or funny hairdos using a sponge dipped in paint. Pasted cotton balls can be used to design the clown's collar and to create a 3-D nose.

When students are finished, have them give their clowns funny names. Display clown faces on your bulletin board with circus cutouts that can include a master of ceremonies, a trapeze artist, elephants and tigers or a person being shot from a cannon.

Monster Necklaces and Ropes

Playing with paper teaches students manual dexterity and hand coordination. Students like to make necklaces, bracelets or ropes of paper and other materials. Use colored thread spools, or have students decorate plain spools, and string them together. Thread spools can also be used as wheels for pull toys. Buttons, flowers, paper designs and popcorn are easily pierced with a threaded needle to create decorative ropes or necklaces. When finished, costume jewelry can be used in class plays or to stage a monster fashion show.

Trees

Another way to teach humor in arts and crafts is to create a funny tree. Tree branches with many twigs can be placed in a pot and anchored with gravel or sand. Students can hang anything on your tricky tree you suggest, including shells decorated with smiles, humorous ornaments, or silly words.

Mobiles

Lighthearted mobiles are easy to make and fun to do. Cover wire hangers with cray paper or foil. Attach two hangers to the edge of one to form the frame on which students can attach happy decorations. Favorite themes include birds, butterflys, flowers, boats, fish, stars, or animals, or you can use pieces of paper bearing students' names.

To create mobiles that make noise in the wind, attach jingle bells to the frame using string or yarn.

Thinking Caps

Students often worry that school assignments will be difficult or impossible to master. One way to take advantage of young imaginations is to construct thinking caps in class. Caps or hats can be made in the shape of a triangle.

Students can decorate their thinking caps and keep them in their desk. When students are anxious about a new lesson, have them put on their thinking caps to help them overcome their fears.

Greeting Cards

We give funny greeting cards to cheer up people, often about an unfortunate situation. We joke when someone is sick to make them feel better, or send a funny birthday card to relieve anxiety about growing older.

Writing humorous greeting cards is a skill that students can learn with practice. Joke writing is not as easy as it seems, as students must write simply and clearly. Jokes in greeting cards use standard joke formats. The *"setup"* appears on the front of the card, with the *"punchline"* inside. (See Chapter 9, "Anatomy of a Joke.") The following exercise lets students make greeting cards for their favorite occasion.

Exercise: *Let students choose a holiday they would like to write about. Have students write a joke setup on the outside of the card and a punchline inside, with funny pictures to illustrate the joke. Holidays include: All occasion, birthday, Christmas, Easter, Father's Day, Friendship, Get Well, Graduation, Grandparent's Day, Halloween, Mother's Day, New Baby, New House, New Year's or Valentine's Day.* Example:

Birthday Card
Cover: Someone like you deserves a million dollars on your birthday.
Inside: How about chipping in to our collection?

Book Writing

Ongoing projects give students a sense of excitement. When students are especially good, bring ongoing projects out of the closet as a treat. Book writing is a typical ongoing craft project.

Books can be about a favorite subject, discussed in a humorous way. Every page will contain description and a picture cut from a magazine, or an illustration by the student. You can divide students into pairs — one to illustrate, and one to write the text; then switch so each child has a book to take home. You can assign students subjects (like, the book of vowels, or, a book of sounds [buzz, whoosh, crash] with pictures illustrating things that make these noises). Other possible book subjects:

My family
My pets
My favorite things
Cars
Pairs (things that come in twos; socks, mittens, hands)
Opposites
Fish
Flowers
Food
My favorite foods
The numbers book
The colors book (write the color on top of the page, and clip out pictures to illustrate.)
Shapes/colors/size
The alphabet book
A book of poems

Bulletin Boards

The joy of arts and crafts comes with the public display of the artwork. When the class creates together, the bulletin board gives everyone a sense of accomplishment and pride in a team effort.

Because bulletin boards take so much space, they also play an important role in setting the mood in your classroom. Monthly themes are often dictated by the holiday schedule, or they can reflect whatever subject dominates your monthly lesson plan. Bulletin boards are also the perfect place to express the mood of a classroom, whether they feel joy or sadness about an important event in their lives.

One way to make sure students are enthusiastic about bulletin boards is to let them decide what the monthly theme and design should be. Teach students responsibility by assigning individuals to bulletin board upkeep.

Bulletin boards should combine words and pictures of different sizes and colors. The largest pieces should draw students in for a closer inspection of the board's theme. Attractive bulletin boards should also make use of various textures, some of them three-dimensional. The organization of a bulletin board's pieces can alternate from geometric or abstract designs from one month to the next.

Since children love to touch things, create an interactive bulletin that invites students to touch and learn about how some things feel. Vocabulary words like "rough" or "soft" can be cut from materials that define them. Aluminum foil can function as a mirror or as an attention-getting shiney surface. Boxes can provide frames for objects that can be removed, studied and replaced by curious students. A bulletin board can also serve as a personal closet hook for 3-D objects like masks or hats used in classroom dramatic exercises.

Since bulletin boards take a lot of time to organize and assemble, you want them to be complex enough to hold the class's interest for several weeks or a month. One way to keep a bulletin board ever changing is to change one part of the board every day, replacing quotes or jokes, for example. This makes the bulletin board something students look forward to from one day to the next.

IV. CLEANUP FUN

There is a childish pleasure in making a mess and adult delight in cleanliness. One way to make sure cleaning is fun is to turn it into a game. You can do this by creating clean-teams with specific assignments and awards for good work. Clean-teams can assign themselves names and choose captains and teammates just like a sports team. Teams of three or four students can then be assigned to individual tasks, from laying out newspapers that protect tabletops to periodic sweeps with a broom.

Chapter 6

LAUGHTER AND ANXIETY

No good work is ever done while the heart is hot and anxious and fretted.

Olive Schreiner (Ralph Iron), 1855–1920

SCHOOLROOM ANXIETY

The jokes we find especially funny reflect the major concerns of our existence. Preschoolers, highly concerned about bowel and bladder control, laugh more at bathroom jokes than adults who have mastered elimination functions. Little children laugh at words like poopy, pee-pee, caca, doody or bumhead that refer to body functions that cause young anxiety. As children master these functions, they usually joke less about them. In the same way, adolescents, nervous about discovering their sexuality, are more likely to feel giddy when they hear *"dirty"* jokes or words.

All students feel a certain amount of anxiety about being smart. For some students, school is the first experience with competition other than sibling rivalry. Students soon learn that knowing the right answer brings reward, while not knowing something can be humiliating. Many students tell jokes or riddles because they feel anxiety about learning and intelligence. Smart jokes make light of students who don't know their lessons:

> Teacher: Who was Karl Marx?
> Student: He was the brother of Groucho.

> Teacher: Where are your tonsils?
> Student: I don't know. They were taken out last summer.

In addition to fears about intelligence, elementary school children worry about physical dexterity. In the competitive environment of the classroom, students tease each other's abilities by crossing their eyes, whistling, sticking out their tongues, trying to rub the stomach and top of the head at the same time, and wiggling ears.

Students can feel anxious about many personal concerns, but most worry about growing up (or being grown up) and about having little control over their lives. Outlets such as Saturday morning cartoons and the circus allow youngsters to laugh at silly adults like infantile clowns, magicians and monster movie program hosts. Puppets often play the role of foolish adults, much to the delight of youngsters who like to feel smarter than the big people who rule their lives.

For students as well as teachers, laughing helps relieve anxiety in specific ways. The benefits laughter has on the human mind and body are reviewed in the next section.

I. The Physiology of Laughter

Laughter usually has a positive effect on the human mind and body. The exception to this rule is violent laughter, which can vibrate the diaphragm too painfully causing "side-splitting" laughter. Belly laughter is uncomfortable if we lose bladder control, which can happen if we can't stop laughing.

In most cases, however, laughter releases tension and brings a state of relaxation or euphoria. The entire body contributes to the pleasant physical experience of a good mood. Muscle spasms and convulsions of the diaphragm cause a cathartic, purged sensation and spiritual calming. Laughter also produces a feeling of elation as the heart rate accelerates and respiration increases. This higher oxygen level and rapid breathing often brings a light-headedness, especially after prolonged laughter.

Higher levels of oxygen in the blood can turn the face red during laughter, contributing to a pleasant glow in the laughing face. During smiling and laughter, muscles around the eyes slightly squeeze the tear ducts. The small amount of fluid released into the eyes causes them to sparkle and sometimes tear.

In fact, crying and laughter are closely related emotions. Sometimes we laugh until we cry. Many people laugh when they are sad. Both happiness and sadness produce tearing which cleans the eyes and releases fluids which may be associated with depression. This would explain why we usually feel better after a good cry.

II. Humor and Test Anxiety

What do students fear most in school? Failure! The kind of failure that is measured in numbers accumulated by taking tests. Whether you use the dreaded essay or confusing multiple choices, tricky true and false questions or a fill-in-the-blank brain teasers, your students are sure to feel anxious as test day approaches.

Every once in a while someone comes up with a new way to educate and test students. Computers that allow students to progress at their own pace are helpful, but you can't have students working on computers all day. Team teaching, private tutoring and Montessori Methods also personalize teaching and learning. But when the classroom is overcrowded and the school is understaffed, it isn't always possible to let everyone work at their own pace.

It's nice to dream about creative and gifted kids, each one developing the skills unique to the individual, without competitive testing. But for most schools, the most practical way to test the progress of a group of diverse students is to use traditional testing methods which test everyone at the same time on the same material. That sets up the competitive environment that causes most test anxiety.

Since students fear failure more than anything else when they take a test, there are two ways to make them feel less anxious about test taking. Teach them how to study and how to take tests. This will make them feel more confident about taking the test and less anxious about the possibility of failure. Humor is a great way to relieve anxiety about testing before, during and after the exam. Here are some tips to help students relieve some of their test anxiety.

- **Review study tips every week,** even making good study habits the theme of a class bulletin board. Remind students often to follow these **Exam Do's and Don'ts.**

DO's

- *Do study a little every day.*
- *Do eat a good meal on test days.*
- *Do get a good night's sleep the night before a test.*
- *Do get to class a little early to review your notes.*
- *Do dress up for an exam.*
- *Do get a drink and use the restroom before a test.*
- *Do bring extra pens and pencils to the test.*
- *Do relax. Try some deep breathing exercises if you feel nervous.*

DON'TS

- *Don't cram or try to "pull an all-nighter."*
- *Don't change routines for an exam.*
- *Don't listen to what other students "heard" about the test.*
- *Don't wear uncomfortable clothes during an exam.*

- The day before the exam **review the test content and format.** Students want to know how many pages to expect, what kinds of questions will be asked and whether or not the test is difficult. To the last question I always joke, "I took it last night and I got an A." It always gets a laugh and relieves some of the anxiety about test fairness.
- **Assure students they will have enough time to take the test.** A lot of anxiety comes from the fear that there won't be enough time to write answers and review the exam when it is completed. Unless you are teaching students how to choose priorities, make the test something that can be done in the allotted time period. Allow slower students to take a special test in two parts.
- **Review exam directions.** Show students the day before the exam how the directions are worded, and have them answer some sample

questions. It makes students feel anxious when you have to review directions on exam day when they are concerned about forgetting the subject matter.

- **Hand students some helpful tips the day before the exam.** It makes them feel you have helped in a concrete way.

Test-Taking Tips

- *Do mark difficult items and come back to them at the end of the test.*
- *Do try to answer every question at least once.*
- *Do pace your time by reviewing the entire test for one minute before the test.*
- *Do allow time at the end of the test to correct silly mistakes.*
- *Don't spend too much time on one question.*
- *Don't leave items blank on a test.*
- *Don't change answers if you only guessed. Your first answer is most likely to be the correct one.*
- *Don't look at other papers. Cheating disturbs other students and you may be copying an incorrect answer.*

- **Provide the optimal environment for test taking.** Students will feel most comfortable in their own seats. Seats should make it impossible for students to be tempted to "borrow" answers from fellow classmates.
- **Tell a joke before the test.** The joke should be harmless so students don't think more about the joke than they do about the test. Tell the joke as you are distributing exams so students don't feel you are wasting their test time with a joke. Avoid jokes that could be interpreted as secret messages hinting at test content.
- **Avoid incorporating humorous items on a test** for several reasons. Some students will see the joke item before other students, and their laughter can be distracting. Some students may worry because they don't understand what's funny. Some won't get the joke because they don't expect something funny on a test.
- **Be the arbitor of fairness during a test.** Avoid interruptions, and give students extra time if a disruption cuts into their test-taking time.
- **Be sensitive to student anxiety when returning exams.** After all, failing the exam is what caused the test anxiety in the first place. Fold exams so grades can be viewed privately, and invite students to speak with you after class if they wish. Never share ridiculous

answers with the rest of the class, or even other teachers. Hilarious answers have a way of getting around.

III. Fear of Public Speaking

Surveys have shown that speech making is the number one fear, even surpassing the fear of flying. It isn't really public speaking that causes all that anxiety. It's the fear of public humiliation, the fear of failure, the fear of making a fool of ourselves. Shy students, and even some not-so-shy ones, can feel extreme anxiety about getting up in front of classmates to speak. Telling a joke can help.

Most people tell jokes because the laughter of approval feels good. When we tell jokes in front of a crowd, all eyes and ears turn to us as we make our way through the joke. As we speak, we fear disapproval and ridicule. We want people to like us when we speak. That's why teaching students to feel confident as joke tellers helps them to overcome the fear of public speaking as well.

The only way students will realize that no one is going to throw tomatoes at them when they stand in front of the class is to let them see how harmless it is. The more students experience what it is like to be on stage, the less they will fear all that might happen to them as they perform before others. Here are a few tips from the experts:

- Fear of speaking before a group has one thing in common with fear of test taking; **preparation is the cure.** Students who prepare for the event are more likely to feel confident.
- Public speakers worry that the audience will know more about their subject than they do. If students "do their homework" they will be the experts. Even if classmates do know information, it is a good skill to **learn to field questions.** After students give their speeches, have them answer three questions from classmates.
- Public speakers need to **establish a rapport with the audience.** One way they do this is to enlist audience participation. Have students tell jokes that require a response from classmates. Knock-knock jokes, light bulb, elephant jokes and riddles all require a class response.
- Some students fear getting in front of classmates because they worry they are not properly dressed. **Teach students to dress for a speech** so they feel good about their personal appearance.

- Even when students are prepared and feel good about their physical appearance, they may feel nervous about making a speech. **Teach them deep breathing exercises.** Have students stand up and stretch and shake their arms to relieve tension before giving their speeches.
- Sometimes, public speakers feel more confident with a prop as a supporting device. **Have students "show and tell" a humorous story using some kind of prop** such as a funny picture or object.
- In longer speeches, entertaining speakers **rely on cue cards** to remind them of stories they want to tell. Have students make cue cards to help them tell five jokes in a row. This exercise will help students who suffer from mental blocks when they get in front of a crowd.
- **Teach students how to use acronyms to recall jokes.** The letters of a word (like P–I–A–N–O) can remind them of the first word in their jokes. Another memory recall trick is to have them write a list of five words that remind them of the jokes they want to tell.
- Another fear public speakers have is that they will stutter or say "ah" and "um" too often as they grapple for words. One way to cure ah's and um's is to **have classmates signal the speaker every time an "um" is uttered.** This can be a fun exercise when the signal from classmates is a funny face.
- One symptom of speech anxiety is that the speaker speaks too rapidly as they try to dash through the assignment. **Have students give a pre-assigned one-minute speech.** Time them until they make the speech last exactly one minute, using a steady rhythm. This exercise teaches students to learn to speak clearly and to know their own speech patterns.
- Finally, it may help to **talk to students about their public speaking fears.** Ask them what is the worst that can happen? Once they realize that everyone feels the same way, they will be more empathetic when fellow classmates make a speech and less nervous about public speaking when it is their turn to speak.

Exercise 1: Impromptu Speech — *The purpose of this exercise is to teach students how to make coherent impromptu speeches. Call students to the front of the class in random order, assigning them a topic to discuss in front of classmates for one minute. Subjects should be of general interest so students need no prior preparation. Sample topics include a favorite sport, a favorite hobby, a favorite pet and so forth.*

Exercise 2: Silly Speech — *A variation of this exercise allows students to make silly speeches on make-believe subjects. For example:*

- *The artistic potential of peanut butter.*
- *Let's make hot pink our school color.*
- *Chickens have rights, too.*
- *My dream vacation in Walawala Land.*

IV. Crisis Humor

However awful it may seem to joke in the midst of a crisis, it is actually a most natural thing in the world. Crisis humor, more than anything, seeks to relieve anxiety about our most painful fears. Sometimes, physicians who deal frequently with death and dying, newspaper reporters on the crisis beat, and soldiers in the heat of combat use crisis humor to distance themselves from the awful reality of their existence.

It seems ironic to laugh when the circumstance calls for just the opposite response. But fear makes us nervous, and sometimes we laugh when we feel afraid or uncomfortable. When we recall that laughing and crying have much in common physiologically, it is more obvious that laughing and crying perform the same function for the human spirit. Laughing and crying alike help us relieve physical and emotional tension in a crisis. Even during funerals, it is not uncommon for people to laugh uncontrollably, to cry hysterically or to mix tears with laughter.

Crisis humor, also called *"black humor,"* laughs at death, the taboo, the awful and the grotesque. Black humor makes light of something we would normally take seriously. In the film *Beetlejuice,* for example, a couple dies and goes to the afterlife. In the movie, people appear in the afterlife as they were at the moment of death. One character, burned to death after smoking in bed, is featured as a charred skeleton, still trying to kick his smoking habit.

Crisis humor is rarely funny in the retelling. Try convincing your friends about the "funny" film, *Eating Raul.* This black comedy recounts the story of a couple who raise the down payment for their dream home by murdering people and selling the remains to a dog food company. The broadway play, *Sweeney Todd,* starring Angela Lansbury, was similarly macabre. In the same way, kids think it's as funny to collect Garbage

Patch Kids cards that show cartoon drawings of kids with exploding heads or festering bodies.

"Sick jokes" use black humor to laugh about things we shouldn't. Remember the "mommy, mommy" jokes? Today's kids are telling the same ones I heard as a child. Example:

> "Mommy, mommy. I don't want to eat any more brains."
> "Shut up and keep eating. A mind is a terrible thing to waste."

Here's another sick joke students have been telling for years.

> Willy knocked on the door and said, "Hey Mrs. Jones, can Johnny come out to play baseball?"
> Mrs. Jones said, "Now you know Johnny doesn't have any arms and legs."
> "I know," Willy said, "but we need someone to play first base."

Actually, the above joke belongs to a whole category of sick jokes about the handicapped, many of which take the form of a riddle:

> What do you call a guy without any arms or legs?
> Matt.

> What do you call a girl without any arms or legs?
> Patty.

In part, students tell sick jokes about handicapped people because they want a reaction. Children tell sick jokes for the same reason they tease zoo animals and pull off the wings of flies. Children are experimenters. They test and probe, and they want others to be amazed or shocked by what they do.

Sick jokes, like bad puns, elicit groans rather than belly laughs. The purpose of some sick jokes is to gross out the listener whose response is to tell the joker something like, *"You're a pig,"* or *"You're disgusting."*

Graveyard Humor

Graveyard humor is a form of black humor which is primarily concerned with death. Hospitals sometimes use graveyard humor in terminal wards and geriatric hospitals to help patients cope with imminent death. Graveyard humor is also very much a part of get-well greeting cards, as are jokes that make fun of the discomforts of hospital life.

A substantial number of graveyard jokes are about dead babies;

> What's the difference between a truck full of bowling balls and a truck full of dead babies?
> You can't stick a pitch fork in the bowling balls.

How do you make a dead baby float?
Two scoops of vanilla ice cream and a cup of root beer.

A popular variation of the dead baby jokes are about deformed babies. These jokes usually use a good news/bad news format as the doctor informs a mother of the tragedy:

A doctor walks into the maternity ward. "I have some good news and some bad news," he said. "The good news is you just gave birth to an eight pound eye." The mother asked, "What's the bad news?"
"It's blind."

You may have also heard students joking about national or international tragedies including the death of beloved political figures or celebrities. Just as some people express grief at a funeral by telling jokes, so too will some students distance themselves during a crisis by making fun of it. Laughing at a tragedy does not necessarily mean a student is insensitive, disrespectful or cruel. What it does mean is that a student does not want to deal with pain or serious feelings. Laughter in a crisis is often a coping mechanism to help students deal with a tragic reality.

We, as teachers, may understand why students tell jokes during a crisis. This does not mean it is any easier to accept insensitive jokes about serious subjects. How do we react to crisis jokes that may hurt other students? As sensibly as possible, and as each situation dictates. Here are a few guidelines:

- **Listen to crisis jokes.** If everyone is telling them, students are indirectly saying they are anxious. Take time to talk about the crisis.
- Too often adults protect children during a crisis, when the kids know exactly what's going on. Don't tell very young students more than they want to know, but **answer student questions as honestly and directly as possible.** They know when you're holding back.
- **Let students speak openly about the crisis.** Be a mediator for everyone's opinion. Letting students know what your opinion is may inhibit students with opposing opinions from expressing their anxiety.
- Young students worry during a crisis that something will happen to the adults they depend on to take care of them. **Be a care-giver during a crisis.** Assure students you will be there for them no matter what happens.
- **Let students express their feelings about the crisis in a fun way,** drawing pictures of their thoughts.

- Another thing that worries students during a crisis is that they are losing control. Stage a humorous puppet show to act out some of the dialogue they have heard. **Help students resolve the situation as they would have liked it resolved using dolls.** This will make them feel like they have more control over the situation.

Chapter 7

LANGUAGE AND LAUGHTER

People laugh at me more because of my eccentric sentences than on account of the subject matter. . . . There is no wit in the form of a well-rounded sentence.

Artemus Ward, 1871

Jokes depend on the ability of words and sentences to be flexible; to rhyme and have rhythm and to have multiple meanings. Jokes also rely on the use of colloquialisms, informal language which is slightly inappropriate or even incorrect. Formal, correct language is less adaptable to joking, except when formality is being made fun of along with less than ideal human qualities like pomposity, pride or snobbery.

Language-based humor depends on many things besides words. It is the way we say things that really causes laughter; a complex combination of verbal and non-verbal noises and gestures. This chapter outlines some of the most important elements of humor in language, suggesting ways students can create humor with words. Exercises allow them to familiarize themselves with plays on words, figures of speech and tricks to create funny sounds and funnier jokes.

I. PRONUNCIATION

From the earliest sounds of infants, we laugh at the noises humans make. We silly adults goad babies with goo-goo and ga-ga noises, and babies make us laugh just by saying da-da-da.

As language becomes more sophisticated, we continue to find humor in sounds. Professional comics know that certain sounds, such as "k," "w" and "p," are more likely to cause laughter than others. The word *"wimp,"* for example, sounds funnier than *"timid."* The word *"Buick"* sounds funnier than *"Chevrolet."*

Humorous pronunciations are an important part of poetry and literary works, both of which use various language devices to cause readers to smile. This section reviews common pronunciation devices used to create humor.

Alliteration

Alliteration is the occurrence of the same initial sound in a phrase or sentence as in Peter Piper picked a peck of pickled peppers. Alliteration is an important joke-telling device because we perceive similar and repetitive sounds as pleasant and funny. Alliteration is commonly used in children's stories because simple repetitive sounds are a delight to kids.

Exercise: *Present students with a list of vocabulary words. Have students show their understanding of alliteration by writing two adjectives for each noun listed. Adjectives should begin with the same letter as the nouns you provide.* Examples:

> **Bear = big black bear**
> **Cat = cute, cuddly cat**

Onomatopoeia

Onomatopoeia is the formation of a word that sounds like its referent. Words like buzz, click, crack, snap, crash, zap, pop, zip, and splash enliven written as well as oral stories.

Sounds are funniest when they are heard out of the expected context. We expect to hear a horse in a barn or on a farm, but not in a school gymnasium. We anticipate classroom sounds, but school noises do not include burps or jungle bird noises from the back of the room. We laugh at sounds heard out of context because they make us feel nervous and unsafe, feelings that laughter relieves.

Exercise 1: *Have students write a brief story using words to describe sounds. Students can present their stories in front of the class, showing their understanding of onomatopoeia by exaggerating the sounds in their reports. Here's a list of possibilities:* **bang, gulp, bing, kerplunk, bong, moo, bow-wow, oink, click, ping, crash, splash, crunch, zap, crack, zip.**

Exercise 2: *Create humorous stories that include sounds made out of context. Students can tell stories that describe dogs barking on the moon, water swishing in the desert or fire crackling underwater.*

Homonyms

Homonyms are words that sound the same, and may be spelled the same, but differ in meaning. Here are some examples:

land — *solid surface of the earth, ground, soil, dirt*
land — *to bring a vehicle to rest on earth, to arrive*

fair — *just, upright, impartial*
fair — *exposition, carnival, bazaar*

Exercise: *Identify the homonyms in the following sentence. Write two definitions for the word or phrase that creates the joke.*

*The famous tailor held a **press** conference.*
*He telephoned the girl next door. It was a **close call**.*
*The politician wrote in **Capitol** letters.*
*The baker's union wants more **dough**.*
*The janitor's union proposed **sweeping** reforms.*
*The man who lit the torch on the Statue of Liberty said it was the **high light** of his career.*
*He cooked the fish on **fry day**.*

*The dentists worked on the **drill team**.*
*He got a **charge** out of the credit card.*
*The Karate Restaurant only serves **chops**.*
*The fireworks were a real **blast**.*
*That school sure is **classy**.*
*The barn was built to give horses a **stable** environment.*

Homophones

Homophones are words that sound the same even though they are spelled differently, as in *there/their/they're, to/two/too* or *"sum"* and *"some."*

Jokes can be created by confusing homophones. Homophone exercises teach students the correct use of a word and also how to manipulate words playfully.

Exercise: *Correct the homophones in the following sentences.*

*What's black and white and **red** all over? (read)*
*No one gets hungry in the desert because of the **sand which** is there. (sandwiches)*
*Mom didn't want the doctors to operate on dad because she doesn't like people to open her **male**. (mail)*

Accents

Most of us recognize classic characteristics of regional and national accents. American regional accents (Brooklyn, Southern, Valley Girl, and Texan, to name a few) as well as foreign accents (British, French, Irish, Indian, Arab, and Oriental) are commonly heard in North American comedy clubs and T.V. sitcoms. Here's a typical joke that pokes fun at accents or pronunciation.

A newcomer to Hawaii asked a cab driver. "I've heard two ways to say the name of your state. Tell me, is it ha-why-ee or ha-vy-ee"
"Ha-vy-ee," said the cab driver.
"Thank you," the visitor said.
"You're velcome," the driver replied.

Accents are an important part of performing impersonations. Reproducing accents requires a good ear for imitation and practicing manipulation of the speech muscles. It's easy to speak with an accent in the mind, but the reproduction that comes out is often very different from the authentic sound of an accent.

One way to reproduce an accent without a true pronunciation is to use words commonly associated with the foreign language or regional accent. When comedians want to speak with a French accent, for example, they pronounce *"the"* as *"zee."* To emulate an Australian accent, use a couple of Aussie words like *"G'day"* or *"mate."* To speak Valley Girl, use in-group language like *"gag me with a spoon,"* and *"tubular."*

There are several age factors involved in a child's ability to discern accents. As with any humorous event, students must master the correct way of saying something before they can appreciate a humorous digression. Simple exaggerations in intonation are most pleasing to the very young. Foreign accents are more complex and require more experience with languages other than the native tongue.

III. MISPRONUNCIATIONS

Since humor usually represents a deviation from the ideal, mispronunciations are more often a part of jokes than not. Mispronunciations come in many forms, from exaggerations in accents or loudness to totally incorrect sounds.

Hyperpronunciations

Hyperpronunciation involves the exaggerated pronunciation of a word. In many cases, hyperpronunciation betrays pomposity as when people pronounce *"tomato,"* *"vase,"* and *"aunt"* with a short "a," than mistakenly pronounce *"potato"* (po-tah-to) using the same rule.

Another type of hyperpronunciation occurs when people interject a foreign accent in the middle of an English sentence. Some people do this to show off their foreign language abilities, but incongruous accents usually sound humorously pompous.

Exercise 1: *Have students hyperpronounce five of their favorite jokes, pretending to have a snob's accent.*

Exercise 2: *Create humor by pronouncing a phrase that contains a word in a non-English language, hyperpronouncing the foreign words as in the following examples.*

The man named Raul came from *Nicaragua.*
The hors d'oeuvres at that French restaurant were magnifique.
The thing I liked best in Japan was the sukiyaki.
The bratwurst at that delicatessen was gút gút gút.

Spoonerisms

Spoonerisms were named after the Rev. William Archibald Spooner, Dean of New College, Oxford, who was known for his slips of the tongue. Spoonerisms are accidental or contrived inversions of sounds, letters, words or phrases which sometimes cause people to say something taboo. For example, there was the usher who wanted to say, *"Let me show you to your seat,"* but said, *"Let me sew you to your sheet."* The Reverend Spooner wanted to say, "We all know what it is to have a half-formed wish inside us," but said instead, "We all know what it is to have a half-warmed fish inside us."

Exercise: *Have students write ten spoonerisms, or let them rewrite spoonerism using correct grammar.*

Malapropisms

A *malapropism* is the mistaken use of a word that sounds similar to the correct one. It is named after an English travel writer, Mrs. Malaprop, who appears in the comedy, *The Rivals,* by Richard Brinsley Sheridan. Mrs. Malaprop often misinterpreted things she heard and saw while traveling in America. Another popular character who used malapropisms was Archie Bunker, whose mistakes often revealed his bigotry and prejudices.

Malapropisms are funny, not only because they expose ignorance, but also because the misuse of "big" words usually reveals a person is trying to impress listeners. There was the man, for example, accused of bigotry who replied, *"I resemble that remark."*

Tongue Twisters

Tongue twisters are groups of words of phonetic similarity which stress the speech apparatus when pronunciation is attempted rapidly. Young students love tongue twisters as they learn to manipulate their mouths and tongues. Here are two of the classics:

Unique New York
Peter Piper picked a peck of pickled peppers.

Speech Defects

Most humorous events involve a contrast between an ideal and a defect. Speech defects such as slurring, stuttering or spitting ("say it, don't spray it") are part of comedy because defective speech contrasts with the ideal. Sometimes we laugh at speech defects because they make us feel anxious and uncomfortable, but also because we feel superior and distanced from the defect. Here's a sick joke that uses a speech defect as a comic device:

> A little boy approached a woman and said, "W-w-were you b-b-born in D–Detroit?"
> "Yes."
> "I-i-in n-n-1949?"
> "Yes, I was."
> "D-d-did you ha-ha-have a m-m-miscarriage?"
> "Why, yes, I did."
> "M-m-mother!"

Students find it playful to imitate speech defects as part of the discovery of mouth muscles and language abilities. In some cases, students forget the difference between making funny sounds with their mouth and making fun of a real human being with a speech defect, a difference we need to explain.

Exercise: *Have students tell jokes that require them to alter their voice to speak with a funny accent (like speaking underwater).*

> What did the elephant say when his trainer cut off his trunk.
> —Very funny. (Hold nose while speaking.)

III. HUMOR AND LANGUAGE

Many jokes are a product of a misuse of grammar. Humorous grammar, like funny pronunciations, are deviations from the ideal.

Grammar and Syntax

Grammar has an obvious role in the creation of humor, in that joke setups and punchlines depend on the listener's knowledge of correct language and sentence patterns. Word order, or "syntax," is an important part of creating humor for the same reason. Recall the sentence that makes fun of this truth: *"A sentence is a terrible thing to end a preposition with."*

Incorrect word order can change the intended meaning of a sentence so that something funny is stated or implied instead. For example, an incorrectly placed clause erroneously attributes action in the sentence to the wrong subject as in the sentence, "One unanswered question is the author of the book."

Exercise: *Write sentences in which the action is attributed to the wrong subject. Have students rewrite the sentences correctly.*

Personification

Personification is the representation of inanimate objects as living beings. Personification can also be a humanizing of non-humans as in *The Animal Farm.* Personification is an important element in the creation of cartoons and children's literature, offering children the opportunity to fantasize about befriending animals, aliens and magical beings like dwarfs and elves.

Personification is also an accepted joke device. We think nothing, for example, of beginning a joke by talking about a duck who walked into a bar or asking, *"What did the doorknob say to the telephone?"* This is because the language of joking allows a suspension of reality for the sake of the joke. Personification is also a means of cueing listeners that a joke is on the way.

Exercise: *Select ten inanimate or non-human objects, or have students write their own list of non-human things. After each object, write down the main qualities of the object. When this is done, have students make up jokes personifying the words on their list. Students should use the outstanding qualities on their list to create double meanings in their jokes.*

Example 1: Lightbulb (bright = intelligent; lights can be "on" or "off")
Sample jokes:

What did the teacher say to the lightbulb?
"You sure are bright."
What did the lightbulb say to the switch?
"You turn me off."

Example 2: Rug (spreads, covers)
What did the Texas rug say to the floor?
"I got you covered, partner."

Fun With Poetry

Among the fun qualities of language is its ability to conform to standard poetic formats. "Poetic license" allows us to accept variation in the order of words to achieve a desired effect.

Creating poetry is one way to allow students to forget about grammatical restrictions they learn in school. Still, conforming even to free verse requires a certain amount of discipline as students fashion poems to predetermined rules of rhyme and meter.

Among the most common structures of student poetry are *lymericks*. Lymericks are easy to create and manipulate. Here's one example:

> *There once was a man from Kalamazoo*
> *Who often dreamed of eating his shoe.*
> *He awoke late one night*
> *In a terrible fright*
> *Now instead of one tongue, he has two.*

Most poetry for young people follows the "Rule of Three R's." Poems rhyme, have rhythm and repetition. Poems or jingles with a humorous punchline teach students to enjoy poetry as a thing of levity and delight rather than as tedious, confusing puzzles.

One way to teach poetry is to sing the verses before you dissect the poem's rhyme, rhythm and repetition. If a poem is not lyrical enough to accompany music, try exaggerating the rhythm, separating the syllables and pronouncing them rhythmically. This is also a good way to memorize a poem. Once the poem is committed to memory, it is easier to divide the individual verses for study and comment.

Once students have learned to recognize a poem, have them write their own verses. You can ask them to put their poetry to music—or have them write a poem to the melody of a favorite song. Music will help students recognize the number of syllables they are allowed to use in a verse. Teach them how to search for rhyming words.

IV. LANGUAGE AND MEANING

Semantics

Semantics is the study of the meaning of words, especially how meaning changes over time. Since the same words can mean different things to different people, we sometimes say that arguments are a question of semantics, or differences in opinion about word choice and meaning.

Etymology

One way to have fun with language is to introduce vocabulary words with their origin or history. For example, the word rubber has its origin in the ability of this substance to rub out pencil marks, a characteristic discovered quite by accident by Joseph Priestly in 1770.

Etymology dictionaries, available in public libraries, provide an endless source of classroom fun. Many dictionaries also provide some word history along with definitions. Dictionary games are a good way to pass the time on rainy days when students can work alone or in teams, racing to discover the word history of your vocabulary list.

Eponyms

Eponyms are words that refer to real or make-believe people whose names have become synonymous with a place, era, institution or practice. *"Romulus,"* for example, is the eponym of *"Rome."*

There are plenty of humorous eponyms that can teach your students the origin of words and help them remember the meaning with an interesting story. Eponym dictionaries are available in public libraries, but here are a few sample eponyms which might be used in a fill-in-the-blank exercise, as a spelling list, or to set up matching columns with which students make correct associations.

Melba toast — *This delectable cracker was named after a famous opera singer while dieting at the Savoy in London. (After Dame Nellie Melba)*

Nimrod — *Synonymous with fool, this man founded the city of Babel.*

Pussyfoot — *A nickname given to an American do-gooder whose catlike abilities helped him pursue people who broke prohibition laws. (After William Eugene "Pussyfoot" Johnson)*

Acronyms

Acronyms are words formed from the letters of a name, the way WAC stands for Women's Army Corps. An acronym can also be formed by taking more than one letter of several words. Radar, for example, stands for radio detecting and ranging.

Abbreviations

It is a natural thing to abbreviate. We make things shorter because it is easier, more economical and less time consuming. Thus we say L.A. instead of Los Angeles, math instead of mathematics and Y.M.C.A. instead of Young Men's Christian Association.

Exercise: *Have students identify the following abbreviations. Then make up new meanings for the abbreviation to create a humorous switch. The switch should contain some truism that exposes the underside of the ideal as in the following examples.*

A.S.A.P. (as soon as possible)
Switch: at some appointed period

C.E.O. (chief executive officer)
Switch: careless, excessive and overbearing

C.O.D. (cash on delivery)
Switch: cheaters owe for goods

C.P.A. (certified public accountant)
Switch: cash profit accumulator

DNA (deoxyribonucleic acid)
M.A. (Magister Artium, master of arts)
M.D. (doctor of medicine)
M.B.A. (master of business administration)
Ph.D. (Philosophiae Doctor, doctor of philosophy)
P.S. (post scriptum, written after)
R.S.V.P. (repondez s'il vous plait)
SALT (strategic arms limitation talks)
V.I.P. (very important person)

Chapter 8

THE AMBIGUITY OF LANGUAGE

A slip of the foot you may soon recover, but a slip of the tongue you may never get over.

Ben Franklin, *Poor Richard's Almanac*

I. THE HUMOR OF DOUBLE-ENTENDRE

Language is a personal, subjective method of communication, often having more than one meaning. We speak of language as having a literal and a figurative interpretation. Literal meanings are the obvious ones, usually the primary meaning of a word or phrase. We sometimes say that a literal expression is delivered verbatum, which means factual and explicit and without exaggeration, metaphor or any other embellishment.

Figurative language, on the other hand, makes use of figures of speech including symbolism, metaphors and hypothetical ideas. Often when we speak figuratively, we don't expect people to take us literally. When a literal message is contained in a figurative joke we can always say we were *just kidding.*

Two-year-olds find it humorous to make up words, or call objects different names. By the age of three, children are beginning to comprehend the ambiguity and the flexibility of literal and figurative language, a linguistic ability that is imperative to the comprehension of most kinds of jokes. Young students are quick to understand simple word ambiguity, as in the following exercise:

> What doesn't break when it falls? (A waterfall)
> What breaks without falling? (A storm, or good news)
> What goes from Toronto to Quebec without moving? (The road, or highway)
> What kind of nail should you never hit with a hammer? (A thumbnail, fingernail or toenail)
> Where can you be sure to find happiness? (In the dictionary)
> What holds water even though it's full of holes? (A sponge)
> What speaks every language in the world? (An echo)
> What two words have more than 1000 letters? (Post Office)
> How many important women have been born in Canada? (None, only babies are born there.)
> How many crackers can you eat on an empty stomach? (One. After that you're not empty.)
> What does everyone use even though it belongs to you? (Your name)
> What can you give to others, but still keep for yourself? (A cold)
> What is difficult to hold, even though it's as light as air? (Your breath)
> What can you never have for breakfast? (Dinner)
> When can you carry water in a net? (When it's frozen)
> What weighs more, a ton of feathers or a ton of rocks? (Neither. They both weigh the same.)
> What has cities but no houses? (A map)
> What has fingers and a thumb without having any skin or bones? (A glove)
> What has a tongue but cannot speak? (A shoe)
> What does the average butcher weigh? (Meat)
> Who wears a bigger hat, a Texan or a Canadian? (The one with the bigger head)
> What lies in a bed but never sleeps? (A garden)
> What kind of fish don't swim? (Fried fish)

By the time students are ten or eleven, they are capable of greater complexity of language. This exercise helps students realize that language has flexibility and that words can have multiple meanings.

Exercise: *What's the difference between? Answer the question: What's the*

difference between, using the cross-rhyming pattern to discover helpful hints.
Examples:

What's the difference between a kitten and a comma?
The Kitten has a claw at the end of its paw.
The comma has (ANSWER: a pause at the end of its clause.)

What's the difference between a wounded lion and a rain cloud?
The lion roars with pain.
The cloud (ANSWER: pours with rain.)

What's the difference between a jeweler and a jailer?
A jeweler sells watches.
A jailer (ANSWER: watches cells.)

What's the difference between a hill and a pill?
The hill is hard to get up.
The pill is (ANSWER: hard to get down.)

What's the difference between a pound of potatoes and a construction worker?
A pound of potatoes weighs a pound.
A construction worker . . . (ANSWER: pounds away.)

What's the difference between a donkey and a postage stamp?
Sometimes it is necessary to lick a donkey with a stick.
Sometimes it is necessary to (ANSWER: stick a stamp with a lick).

What's the difference between a thief and a church bell?
A church bell peals from the steeple.
A thief (ANSWER: steals from the people).

What's the difference between a train conductor and a teacher?
The conductor minds the train.
The teacher (ANSWER: trains the mind).

What's the difference between a hungry man and a greedy man?
The hungry man longs to eat.
The greedy man (ANSWER: eats too long).

Oxymoron

Oxymoron is the use of opposites which seem to contradict each other as in *"successful failure"* or *"rich pauper."* Mark Twain was a master of oxymoron. He once said, *"It usually takes more than three weeks to prepare a good impromptu speech."* Artemus Ward, another master oxymoronic, said, *"Let us be happy and live within our means, even if we have to borrow the money to do it."*

Exercise: Have students write ten oxymoronic phrases. Here are some more examples to get them started.

She drove the car in a straight circle.
He was a professional amateur.
She was born old.
It's a definite possibility.

Synonyms

Synonyms are words that mean the same thing, the way *"huge"* means almost the same thing as *"big"* or *"giant."* For every serious word there is a humorous synonym with a similar or exact meaning. Professional comics often use humorous synonyms to uncover the truth behind a word or phrase, or to interpret language in a funny way.

Exercise: *Have students think of a humorous synonym for your list of vocabulary words.* Examples:

inexpensive (cheap, junky)
large (monstrous, industrial)
corpulent, obese (fat, bloated)

Euphemisms

Courtesy in educated society requires us to say things in a *"nice"* way. Euphemisms are words or expressions we use in place of something more direct, explicit or potentially offensive to listeners, as when polite women say they need to "powder their noses" to avoid saying they have to urinate.

Professional comedians sometimes create humor by replacing euphemisms with their true meaning or misinterpreting a euphemism that might be interpreted in various ways.

Exercise: *Have students write as many euphemisms as they can for your list of vocabulary words. Students should write their synonym lists from the most to least euphemistic word. Note the euphemism is the most polite way to express the word.* Examples:

comedian *(jester, buffoon, fool, joker, clown)*
misguided *(misled, confused, lost, out-of-it)*
unwise (witless, ignorant, brainless, stupid, idiotic)
humorous *(funny, hilarious, cracked, goofy)*
mad *(demented, neurotic, crazy, lunatic, idiotic)*
tall tale *(falsehood, untruth, fib, lie)*
leisurely *(sluggish, gradual, leaden, slow, dead)*

idle *(passive, sluggish, lazy, loafing)*
unsightly *(plain, homely, repulsive, ugly, revolting)*

As a variation to this exercise, present students with a list of words and have them circle the most polite, euphemistic one.

Cliches and Sayings

A cliche is a trite or overused expression. B–Western movies are full of cliches like, *"Let's head 'em off at the pass."* Catchwords or catch phrases are trendy expressions that come and go with temporary fads.

The language of humor is possible because communication is predictable, full of cliches and formalized exchanges. All moms, for example, end up telling their kids things like, "Don't run or you'll fall and break your leg," or "Don't cross your eyes or they'll stay that way." Most language-based humor depends on stereotypical language that everyone recognizes and uses on a daily basis.

Before students can use cliches to create their own jokes and punchlines, they need to learn to recognize cliches. This is sometimes hard to do because cliches are so prevalent that we hardly recognize them as such. Too often people resort to cliches to communicate instead of searching inward for *"le mot juste,"* the more precise word or phrase.

In many cases, you will need to point out that an expression is a cliche, especially when it is a common expression. Once students recognize cliches, they can alter them to create a humorous contrast.

The following exercise is designed to teach students to recognize and then make use of cliches to create jokes.

Exercise: *List ten cliches. Have students alter the cliche to create a humorous alternative.* Examples:

*You can't **fight** City Hall.*
*You can't **right** City Hall.*

That's a whole new ball game.
So far, so good.
Actions speak louder than words.
He doesn't have a leg to stand on.
Just keep a stiff upper lip.
It's a bit off the beaten path.
Hold your horses.
Just grin and bear it.

He'd give you the shirt off his back.
She meant it from the bottom of her heart.
He followed in the footsteps of fame.
That's a real feather in his cap.
Heroes have feet of clay.
She was dressed to kill.
Let's cross that bridge when we come to it.
She cried all the way to the bank.
He was born with a silver spoon in his mouth.
He's too big for his britches.
That just scratches the surface.
He has a good track record.
She was fighting an uphill battle.

Another type of language convention is the saying. Adages, maxims, and proverbs are phrases that contain words of wisdom as in *"It is better to give than to receive,"* or *"a rolling stone gathers no moss."* Sayings can be humorous when they are incorrectly stated or stated at an inappropriate time as in, *"It is better to give a rolling stone than to receive moss."*

Some jokes make use of sayings by rewriting them as puns as in the following joke:

Once there was an African king who was worried someone might steal his throne. For this reason, he hid the huge chair in his attic. One day, while sitting in his grass hut, the throne came crashing onto his head and killed him. The moral? People who live in grass houses shouldn't stow thrones.

Exercise: *Have students write jokes by rewriting the following sayings as punchlines:*

Tis better to give than to receive.
You can't teach an old dog new tricks.
The grass is always greener on the other side.
A stitch in time saves nine.
The early bird gets the worm.

Similes

A simile is a figure of speech in which two unlike things are compared. This comparison is usually introduced with the words "like" or "as." Many similes are so common they have become cliches as when we say we're *as hungry as a lion* or *as blind as a bat.*

Simile Exercise: *Mix the list of correct answers. Have students match the columns.*

As big as (a house)
As pretty as (a picture)
As tall as (a tree)
As hungry as (a lion, a bear)
As tough as (nails)
As hot as (an oven)
As cold as (ice)
As wet as (water)
As sharp as (glass)
As sour as (a lemon)
As ugly as (sin)
As delicate as (a flower)
As thin as (straw, a rail, a toothpick, a stringbean)
As blind as (a bat)
As clean as (a whistle)
As poor as (a church mouse)
As light as (a feather)
As clever as (a fox)
As quiet as (a mouse)
As deaf as (a doorknob)
Cooler than (a cucumber)
Heavier than (a lead balloon)
As happy as (a lark)
As cute as (a button)

Metaphors

A metaphor is a figure of speech in which the meaning of something is transformed from the object it usually designates to another idea. This creates a new and unusual comparison. We might say, for example, that young people are in the *"spring"* of their lives while the elderly are in the *"winter"* of their lives.

Life is full of metaphors, from the simplest of comparisons to complex "high" ideas. Metaphors are a great way to teach students the abstractions implied in language and speech.

We live in a fast-paced, complex world in which few people *"stop to smell the roses."* Students can be taught to *"sense"* the world around them by concentrating on their sense of sight, touch, smell, and hearing in the creation of metaphors. Metaphor exercises help students understand the higher, abstract concepts that exist between things and the ideas they evoke.

Metaphor Exercise: *The following objects have unique qualities. Have students think of words to describe the objects. (It may help to close eyes to isolate the sensation they are trying to describe.)*

Think of:

(a) a person you're reminded of
(b) a place you are reminded of
(c) a thing you are reminded of
(d) a feeling you are reminded of

Associated with the following:

SMELL

Mint is like . . .
A Rose is like . . .
Clover
Garlic

TOUCH (Texture)

Sandpaper is like . . .
Silk
Dandelions

SIGHT

Red
Black
White
Yellow
Children
Kittens

HEARING

Scratching
Classical Music
A Lullaby

TASTE

Bitter
Sweet
Sour
Tart
Spicy

Metaphor-Cliche Exercise: *In this more advanced exercise, have students use cliches and metaphors to create jokes.* **Example:** *What do you call a woman with eyes in the back of her head? (Answer: A sight for four eyes).*

The above riddle actually contains two metaphor-cliches. We say people *"have eyes in the back of their heads"* when they are observant We say a person is a *"sight for sore eyes"* when we are glad to see them. In this example we altered one of the metaphors to produce a humorous switch.

It Goes Without Saying

Sometimes we create jokes by stating the obvious. For example, there was a woman in an uncomfortable social situation who asked a man, *"What shall I call you, Dave?"* Then there was the little boy said to his mother, *"I'm sure glad you decided to call me Joey cause that's what everyone else calls me too."*

Exercise: *Have students write ten jokes in which they state the obvious as in the following examples.*

- *How old is that five-year-old?*
- *How tall is that six-foot man?*
- *Do you know what state Dallas, Texas is in?*

Another form of jokes in this category state something twice, but imply that the speaker doesn't know what something means. For example:

- *He's not only frugal, he doesn't like to spend money.*
- *He's not only prejudiced, he has all these preconceived ideas about people.*
- *He not only procrastinates, he puts everything off.*

Exercise: *Give students ten vocabulary words. Show they know what they mean by writing jokes that restate the obvious as in the above examples.*

A third way to say something that doesn't need to be said is to restate the same word twice. Public speakers often do this to emphasize a point, but people are also redundant because some repetitive expressions are cliches or accepted expressions. For example, we may speak of an *"enormous giant,"* or *"hopeful optimism"* or of a *"new innovation."* We tell students to *"observe my watching."* We often begin a sentence saying, *"I myself...,"* when we don't really need to.

Exercise: *Have students write ten sentences in which they use redundancy to emphasize a point in a humorous way.*

A more advanced exercise uses obvious truths to make an ironic statement. For example, *"How come poor people never have any money?,"* or *"How come fat people are always on a diet?"*

Exercise: *Write ten sentences that state the obvious as in the following sentences.*

What happens when you throw a yellow hat into the Red Sea?
It gets wet.

What did Frankenstein say when he stubbed his toe?
Ouch.

If a prince marries a commoner, what does she become?
His wife.

Making Sense of Nonsense

Not everything we express as language makes sense; some of it is *"nonsense."* Nonsense is anything that means nothing as well as something that is perceived as absurd, ridiculous, or foolish. Moms tell their kids something is *nonsense* when it is insignificant.

Nonsense language is created in many ways. When infants try to communicate, they make perfect sense in baby talk, but it sounds like gibberish to everyone else. Some people babble nonsensically after taking drugs that affect the brain, as a result of brain damage or mental illness.

Nonsense is something we can speak on purpose as well. We speak nonsense any time we don't want to be understood, the way politicians sometimes do. Lying children, double-talkers and fast-talking con artists can mix nonsense with enough real language to convince victims to succumb to their charms.

Sometimes people say something that makes no sense at all, if anyone took the time to think about it. This is especially true when we speak in cliches, misstating them. For example, there are two sayings that refer to lost causes:

1. *That's water under the bridge.*
2. *That's water over the dam.*

Sometimes people confuse these sayings and say things like:

1. *That's water over the bridge.*
2. *That's water under the dam.*

Most of us are so accustomed to speaking with cliches and sayings, we only half hear what someone says. Even when someone speaks nonsense, we usually know what they meant to say, so it hardly matters. But students can create their own humorous sayings by purposely mismatching well-known adages.

Exercise: *Take the following sayings and misquote them to create a humorous nonsense expression. Students must use the most recognizable element in the saying for this to be effective.* Example:

1. He's just a wolf in sheep's clothing.
2. He's all thumbs.
Nonsense = "He's all thumbs in sheep's clothing."

As a variation to this exercise, give students a composition incorporating as many of the following sayings as possible. Have them underline each saying; then have them substitute the cliches with their own words.

> To add insult to injury
> To bark up the wrong tree
> To be as blind as a bat
> To be for the birds
> To look a gift horse in the mouth
> To have half a mind to
> To like them apples
> To make a long story short
> To mind one's P's and Q's
> To be off your rocker
> To be as sick as a dog
> To be too good to be true
> To vanish into thin air
> To make a silk purse out of a sow's ear
> To teach an old dog new tricks

II. NON-VERBAL COMMUNICATION

Most verbal jokes rely on *non-verbal communication* or *body language* for a more powerful effect. Body language includes the gestures of our hands as well as general physical movement, our demeanor and facial expressions. Body language is also communicated in the style of our hair, in our clothing and in belongings or props we use when we speak.

Many simple jokes told by grade school students make use of gestures. Young students are proud of their new manual dexterity and their ability to tell riddles using hands. Gesture jokes serve the same function as tongue twisters in that they let students create humor by practicing a new skill. *"What's this?"* jokes require the student to gesture with hands while posing a riddle about the meaning of the hand signal. For example, press the fingers of each hand together several times. This is supposed to be a spider on a mirror, or a spider doing pushups on a mirror.

It's amazing how little most of us know about our own bodies and facial expressions. The following exercise is designed to help students realize how they look when they move their bodies as they speak.

Exercise: *Have students tell some of their favorite gesture jokes.* Example:

> **How do you know there's an elephant in bed with you?**
> **The buttons on his pajamas are this big.** (Hold arms far out to each side.)

Contagious Smiles and Laughter

Smiles and laughter have something in common with yawns in that they are contagious. In comedy clubs, managers seat audience members together because infectious laughter helps people feel comfortable about being expressive.

On television talk shows, cameras often show laughing audience members to prove to viewers that the show is funny. Contagious laughter is the motivation behind laugh tracks on television. Laugh boxes tell us when a joke is supposed to be funny. This is not to say we could not judge how funny a joke is for ourselves. However, seeing and hearing other people laugh makes us laugh more than we would if we heard a joke by itself.

Chapter 9

ANATOMY OF A JOKE

My way of joking is telling the truth. That is the funniest joke in the world.

George Bernard Shaw

I. JOKE CONSTRUCTION

This chapter reviews the nature of jokes, detailing the structure of standard joke formats. Exercises teach students to create their own jokes and to recognize successful joke structure and format.

Setups and Surprise

Funny jokes succeed because they contain an element of surprise. The surprise element in a joke causes intellectual delight by tricking the mind. Children laugh at simple jokes because the humor is new and still surprising. Adults need increasingly complex jokes to challenge more mature and experienced minds.

Surprise in jokes is achieved by *"setting up"* a sense of expectation, then shifting gears with some unexpected reply. This is achieved with a *"setup,"* followed by a *"punch line."* The purpose of the setup is to cause expectation in the mind of the listener. The punch line foils expectation with a surprising twist. This is called *"switching."* Here's one example:

> SETUP: **Last night I had a dream I was in a boat with Dolly Parton.**
> —**Really? How did it go?**
> PUNCH LINE: **Great! I caught a ten-pound bass.**

Unless you heard this joke before, you probably thought the man in the joke was going to tell us if he scored with Dolly Parton, not how he did fishing. This kind of joke succeeds precisely because our thought processes are predictable.

Joke setups are best when they are told confidently. Never say . . .

- *"I'm not very good at telling jokes." Never tell your audience that you are not a good joke teller. It sets them up to be disappointed no matter what you say.*
- *"You've probably already heard this joke, but here goes anyway. . . . " This does nothing but detract from the setup itself. Just tell the joke and don't apologize beforehand.*
- *"Just interrupt me if you've heard this joke before." This kind of invitation is asking someone to stop you in the middle of the joke. The only way a listener can be sure they haven't heard a joke is to hear the punch line or end of the joke. Your punch line may surprise them even if they think they've heard the joke before.*
- *"You probably won't think this joke is funny, but I'll tell it anyway." Let the listener be the judge of a joke's humor. Telling a listener how they will react to your joke is inhibiting.*

Cue the Listener

Sometimes, students don't expect a teacher to tell a joke. Even after you've delivered a well-placed punch line, they may look at you as if you've just arrived from Mars. One way to set up a joke expectation is to use recognizable setups. Among these:

- *Did you hear the one about...*
- *That reminds me of a funny story...*
- *It's like the old saying...*
- *It's funny you should ask...*
- *A funny thing happened on the way to school today...*

Punch Lines

Punch lines are supposed to do what they describe: *"punch"* the psyche with some surprise. Let's see how the joke process works in jokes that appeal to young children. Consider the following examples. First read the joke setup. Consider the logical response? Note how the punch lines could surprise young students.

> **What does a leopard have that no other animals has?**
> (Students expect the answer to be "spots".)
> **Answer: baby leopards**
>
> **How did the woman make sure the fish didn't smell?**
> (Students expect she wrapped the fish in plastic.)
> **Answer: She cut off its nose.**
>
> **Why was the mouse afraid to come out in the rain?**
> (Students expect the mouse was afraid of getting wet.)
> **Answer: Because it was raining cats and dogs.**

Some jokes take advantage of listeners who are skilled at guessing punchlines. Take any old joke, rewrite the punch line, and you are likely to fool listeners who are anticipating the original joke.

Let's take the age-old joke, *"Why did the chicken cross the road?"* This question cues the brain that a joke is expected because it is an absurd kind of riddle, causing listeners to seek a humorous punch line. Everyone expects a logical answer . . . that the chicken crossed the road to get to the other side. Variations of this joke, however, surprise listeners by switching the punch line with lines like, *"the chicken crossed the road because it was too far to walk around."*

Conversely, jokes can be created by switching an expected humorous punch line with a logical response.

> **How do you get to Carnegie Hall?**
> **(Expected response) Practice, man. Practice.**
> **(Switch) Take the A-train to 54th Street.**

Exercise: *(Switcheroos) — Have students write ten of their favorite really old jokes. Then let them rewrite the punch lines to fool classmates with variations.* Example:

> **Why did the chicken cross the road?**
> **Predictable Answer — To get to the other side.**
> **Variation: Why did the kids cross the playground?**
> **Surprise Answer: To get to the other slide.**

Sample old jokes:

> **Customer: Waiter! There's a fly in my soup.**
> **Waiter: That's okay. We won't charge you extra.**

> **Why did the man throw the alarm clock out the window?**
> **He wanted to see time fly.**

> **Doctor, after the surgery will I be able to play the piano?**
> **Sure.**
> **Great! I never could before.**

The next joke illustrates a more complex form of joke setup, in that it requires interaction with the listener. The joker in this case asks a series of questions which sets up a chain of expectation in the listener. Just as this occurs, the joker pulls a switch and fools the listener with the punchline.

> **Q1: What's yellow and goes "dingdong"?**
> **A1: A yellow dingdong.**
>
> **Q2: What's blue and goes dingdong?**
> **A2: A blue dingdong.**
>
> **Q3: What's green and goes dingdong?**
> **A3: A green dingdong?**
> **PUNCH LINE: No—dingdong's only come in yellow and blue.**

Exaggeration and Understatement

The most frequent cause of laughter is the perception of an incongruity. Something is incongruous when it is interpreted as being in an unusual or unexpected combination with something else. While we don't always laugh every time we see two things that do not correspond logically or harmoniously, most amusing situations contain some absurdity.

In many cases, incongruities are exaggerations of some expected image, word or event as in the following example:

> **Why is a policeman the strongest man in the city?**
> **He can stop traffic with one hand.**

Contrast

Throughout the school years we teach students how to organize information logically. However, appreciating humor calls for an ability to recognize when something does not mesh logically with something else. Most jokes are funny because they divert from some ideal. Humorous teachers in Hollywood films, for example, are everything teachers are not supposed to be.

In the film, *Teachers*, Mr. Styles is an emotionless bore whose most notable accomplishment is that he won three consecutive awards for *"most orderly teacher."* His students are so well trained that they move about in class like robots, finishing assignments and turning in papers without any teacher interaction. Mr. Styles' class is so orderly, in fact, that when he dies of a heart attack in class one day, the class continues to function perfectly well without him. Now *that's* funny.

Not all contrasts against the ideal are humorous. Still, we often laugh when we see two things that do not appear to be logical together. For example, kids find it funny to play with Mr. and Mrs. Potato Head, in part, because vegetables aren't supposed to have faces. Teaching students how to have a sense of humor includes lessons that heighten their awareness of contrasts.

Exercise: *Have students create humor by pairing illogical things. Use magazine photos to make the switch between what is expected and what is unexpected. Put a cabbage on a human body, turn a mountain upside down, or paste a dog on top of a pool of water. The purpose of this exercise is to make students more aware of humorous contrasts.*

Conciseness

Preschoolers tell jokes and funny stories on impulse. These early attempts at humor are closely associated with the child's immediate moments rather than an ample repertoire of memories, which they do not yet possess. Since preschoolers have not yet mastered joke-telling skills, they are likely to ramble, to include irrelevant information, to leave out important details and to forget the punch line by the time they reach the end of the joke. Preschoolers also have a short attention span so they may become distracted before they ever finish their funny stories.

Grade school students take longer to perceive the humor of an ambiguous or incongruous event because their cognitive abilities are still immature. As we mature, we *"get"* jokes faster either because we have had experience with a joke format (like riddles or knock-knock jokes), or because our cognitive abilities allow us to guess multiple possibilities as a child cannot yet do.

Because the mind is so quick to set up expectations, joke setups and punch lines must be concise to succeed. Jokes that ramble too long allow the mind to guess the punch line. This is called *"telegraphing."* Guessing a punch line or hearing a joke we already know ruins the surprise and lessens the humorous experience.

Note how concise the language is in the following jokes. Not one word is wasted; not one word needs to be added or eliminated to achieve maximum effect.

> **What's black when it's clean, and white when it's dirty?**
> **A blackboard.**

> **How did the man make his jumping frog fast?**
> **He didn't feed it.**

> **What do poor people have that rich people want?**
> **Nothing.**

Exercise: *Have students bring in a favorite newspaper cartoon, with the caption cut away. Students exchange cartoons and make up humorous captions for them. Remind them that the cartoon drawing shows who is speaking in the caption. There is no "right" or "wrong" answer as long as students follow the rules for joke telling as described in this chapter.*

—State the unexpected—

—Be brief—

—Exaggerate—

Playfulness

In the joke about why the chicken crossed the road, both the joke teller and the listener realize a playful language event is taking place. Everyone understands that the joker didn't really want to know why the chicken crossed the road. The joker and listener simply agreed to suspend reality for just a moment in order to have an absurd language exchange.

Not all setups cue the listener to a playful speech event. Telephone pranks set up the victim to believe the conversation is a serious one, then switch the expected reply. For example:

SETUP: Is your refrigerator running?
STANDARD ANSWER: Yes, I think so.
SWITCH: Then you'd better go catch it.

SETUP: Is your T.V. on?
STANDARD ANSWER: Yes it is.
SWITCH: How does it fit?

Some telephone pranks set up a chain of expectation with multiple phone calls just as some jokes require more conversation than others. One popular prank requires several people to call one number to ask for John or Mary. Later, John or Mary calls to find out if there are any messages.

Telephone pranks give callers power over their adult victims since the jokers usually remain anonymous. Perhaps it is not surprising that telephone joking is most common among teenagers. Future technology may eliminate some of the anonymity of telephone pranks by displaying the joker's phone number on a screen. The technology already exists, created to eliminate harassing or obscene calls. By the time that technology is widespread, teenage pranksters will undoubtedly devise some other means of bothering adults by phone.

People need to perceive that a situation is playful and that it is okay to laugh. Since *disruptive* laughter in the classroom is forbidden, it is sometimes necessary to create a playful mood so students realize adult teachers have given permission to laugh.

One way to teach students that it's okay to be playful is to give them exercises that allow them to be silly. Here's an exercise that does just that.

Silliness Exercise: *Have students write or tell silly jokes like the following examples.*

Why did the hummingbird hum?
He didn't know the words to the song.

What weighs 4000 pounds, has feathers and sings like a bird?
A two-ton canary.

II. JOKE FORMATS

A joke is defined as an amusing story or jesting remark, as a mischievous trick or prank, or as anything perceived as ludicrous to a situation. Joking may mean "teasing" as when we "make fun" of something. Jokes can be witticisms, quips, puns or anecdotes, as long as they are meant to be or perceived as amusing. This section reviews some of the most common joke forms and reviews what's behind the fun they create.

Puns

A *pun* is a *"play on words."* Puns pretend to confuse similar sounding words or multiple uses of the same word as in *Shakespeare (or Wordsworth) ode everything to his publisher.*

Exercise: *Write ten sentences which contain potential puns. Underline all words that might have a similar sounding word or possible homonym. Have students rewrite the sentences to create puns.* Examples:

What happened when the cow didn't come home?
It was an utter disaster. (udder)

Why didn't the cow come home?
He couldn't find his way? (whey)

Why didn't the psychiatrist get the job?
He was too young. (Jung)

Tom Swifties

As students master the parts of speech, they begin to experiment with the possibilities language allows. Tom Swifties, named after the Tom Swift series of children's books, makes humorous use of adverbs as in *"I just love the cheese, she said sharply."*

Exercise: *Have students create 20 Tom Swifties. This large number should exhaust their repertoire of Tom Swifties they already know and force them to think up a few of their own. Here are a few more examples:*

What a beautiful night, she said darkly.
I love my new coat, she said warmly.

I'll have a milkshake, he said coldly.
You're a snake, she rattled.
You're an insect, he buzzed.

Sports Jokes

Jokes create humor by exaggerating or understating reality. This is especially true of sports jokes whose subjects are based on stereotypical ideas about athletes, games and fans. In the following joke, for example, humor is created by exaggerating team loyalty as fanaticism.

It was the biggest game of the season and every seat was taken but one. A man approached and asked a man next to it about it.
"That seat was for my wife," the man said. "We used to come here every year, but then she passed away."
"Couldn't you ask a friend?" the first man asked. "That's one of the best seats in the stadium."
"I would have," the second man replied, "but everyone I know is at the funeral."

A common theme in sports jokes is based on the prejudice that athletes are handsome but stupid. Here are some examples:

What's the average age of a football player from XXX team?
—35. They get them right out of high school.

What's the first thing a basketball player from XXX team does when he gets out of the shower?
—He takes off his uniform.

Did you hear about the baseball player who took his tie back because it was too tight?

Competition Jokes

The laughter of triumph is an important part of victory humor. Humor is a socially acceptable way to be aggressive and hostile about a sporting or competitive event. Competitive laughter tends to be boisterous, expressive and openly derisive.

Laughing at another team, another school, or rival students makes students feel superior and encourages them to win. Competition jokes are full of contempt, sarcasm and loathing. This kind of joking arouses school loyalty and enthusiasm. It also purges students of hostile feelings that might otherwise become violent and physical.

Jokes about rival groups are predictable and formulaic. It doesn't matter who the rival school is; fill-in-the-blanks and the insults are the same. While there are restrictions on laughing at classmates, competition jokes freely make fun of the ignorance of rival players and the ugliness of rival school girls.

Q: What do you call a student from _____ school who has half a brain?
A: A genius

Q: Do you know why _____ school uses astroturf on their playing field?
A: So the cheerleaders won't eat the grass

Q: What do you call a pretty girl from _____ school?
A: A visitor

Q: What do you have when you have a room full of students from _____ school?
A: A full set of teeth

Exercise: *Have students write five jokes about their favorite rival. Competition jokes can make fun of intelligence and beauty, but should not contain racist remarks.*

Light Bulb Jokes

Most light bulb jokes are used to tell ethnic and gender jokes. The original light bulb joke meant to reveal how ignorant an ethnic group was by proposing it was a major effort for people from the group to screw in a light bulb. **Example:**

How many XXXX does it take to screw in a light bulb?
Answer: 100; one to hold the light bulb and 99 to turn the house around.
Variation: 3; one to hold the light bulb and 2 to turn the ladder around.

Light bulb jokes offer an opportunity to make fun of a rival school's education or students as in the following example.

How many students from XXXX school does it take to screw in a lightbulb?
—One. And they get a degree in engineering for doing it.

Most light bulb jokes rely heavily on stereotypes about ethnic groups and gender typing. Example:

How many Jewish American Princesses does it take to screw in a light bulb?
—Two; one to hold the bulb and the other to call daddy.

How many Jewish mothers does it take to screw in a light bulb?
—None; we'll just sit here in the dark.

Some light bulb jokes are rather ingenious at catching the essence of something, even without ethnic or sexist stereotypes.

How many pessimists does it take to screw in a light bulb?
—None. What's the use of trying.

How many surrealists does it take to screw in a light bulb?
—Fish.

How many bullies does it take to screw in a light bulb?
—What's it to you?

Exercise: *Using the above examples, have students write ten light bulb jokes. Jokes should catch the essence of the group they describe without using offensive slurs or stereotypes.*

Elephant Jokes

Elephant jokes often use personification to joke about human behavior. Among the most popular of elementary and adolescent joke forms, some elephant jokes are just plain silly:

How do you know an elephant has been in the fridge?
—Footprints in the Jello.

The elephants in elephant jokes represent something big, powerful and fearful. It is easier to joke about things we fear vicariously, as in an elephant joke, than to discuss taboo subjects openly. We tell elephant jokes for the same reason we tell other kinds of jokes; to disguise the true content in order to approach forbidden subjects, as in the following examples.

How do you know there's an elephant in bed with you?
You can smell the peanuts on his breath.

How do you know an elephant has used your bathroom?
The toilet won't flush.

Exercise: *Have students write and tell ten elephant jokes. They can rely on other jokes they know (such as chicken jokes) and modify them using the elephant and an absurd perspective. (Example: Why did the elephant cross the road? Because his mother told him he could.)*

Good News/Bad News

Another popular joke format uses the *"good news/bad news"* setup. The good news usually sets up a fearful expectation followed by some awful truth or absurdity. For example:

The good news is that your brother just broke an Olympic record for the triple somersault dive.
The bad news is that there wasn't any water in the pool at the time.

Some good news jokes give the bad news first, then reverse the fortune with a positive statement. For example:

The bad news is my brother married a maid.
The good news is, she does windows.

Not all good news/bad news jokes use black humor, but many of them do because the format makes it so easy.

Exercise: *Have students make up ten good news/bad news jokes. Their answers should reflect some irony that cancels or alters the good news.*

Tall Tales and White Lies

The definition of a *"white lie"* is a lie we justify because we want to spare someone's feelings, usually our own.

The practice of telling tall tales is practically a tradition in North America, arriving with those rugged scoundrels called ancestors. Early settlers, explorers and trackers found great humor in preying on gullible visitors from Europe, telling exaggerated stories about the whiskey drinking, uneducated, wild people who inhabited the territories. And that was just the women folk!

Mark Twain was a master of tall tales. He once wrote a newspaper article about a man who invented an air-conditioned suit and froze to death when he tried it out in the desert. Then there was the man who was completely scalped by an Indian, yet was able to ride back to town, holding his scalp above his head. That article appeared in newspapers across the country before someone realized that the story was preposterous.

Sometimes we refer to people who tell tall tales as *yarn spinners*, since they weave their tale ever so slowly, preying on the fears, beliefs, superstitions, ignorance and gullibility of their listeners.

Injecting a bit of truth as part of the joke setup is imperative to good lying. Professional comics often begin their jokes saying, *"this is a true story,"* or *"this actually happened to me."* Convincing listeners they are hearing the truth is an effective way to shock them with a humorous punchline.

Exercise: *Have students write a tall tale. Their story should begin with* *something truthful, play on the fears of listeners, and gradually exaggerate those fears with impossible details.*

III. CRACKING JOKES

Have you ever wondered why some people tell better jokes than others? Some people can tell a joke that isn't particularly funny in itself, but is hysterical because it is told in a certain way.

Successful joke telling has much to do with *"delivery,"* a skill that encompasses many things. Good delivery requires students to use appropriate gestures, a proper *"setup,"* and a good *"punchline,"* stated at just the right moment. Good delivery also depends on a good sense of *"timing."*

Using the standard joke formats discussed in this chapter, students are now ready to perform their jokes for classmates. Perhaps surprisingly, the purpose of joke-telling exercises is not to make classmates laugh, but to understand the dramatics of joke telling.

Memorizing Jokes

Good comics memorize their jokes. They tell them and retell them until they achieve the desired effect in audience members. The same is true of good class clowns. Once they learn a joke or riddle, they will tell it over and over, not realizing that they are getting better at joking with each retelling.

Professional comics memorize their jokes to such an extent that it seems as if they are speaking *"off the cuff."* In the same way, joke-telling exercises should require students to memorize their jokes and to practice them with friends and family members before performing before their peers. Memorizing jokes allows students to practice good study habits in a fun way.

To be most challenging, students should be given several jokes to tell at one time. Have them order their jokes in some kind of pattern around a specific theme such as school or sports. As they move from one joke to the next, the subject matter should flow naturally, as if they are having a conversation with a single person rather than with a group.

Projection

Whenever we speak, we project, creating an image in the mind of the listener by the force and tone of our voice. Projection includes voice inflection, intonation and pitch as well as gestures and other forms of non-verbal communication. Effective projection also means that students speak clearly and loudly enough for everyone to hear them.

Projection often determines whether or not a word or sentence is interpreted as humorous. When we emphasize certain words and specific syllables, we signal deeper meaning behind words. For example, we may say one thing but project a different meaning when our voice tone or body language emphasizes something else.

Intonation and Emphasis

Intonation is the use of various voice tones or "pitches" which measure the frequency, loudness or intensity of speech. When we raise or lower our voices, our intonation tells listeners what we want to emphasize in a sentence. In ancient Latin, emphasis was indicated by moving the most important word to the end of the sentence. In English, we emphasize by raising our tone of voice and speaking louder.

Learning to emphasize words correctly is a normal part of language acquisition. In the same way young children make grammatical errors, they often emphasize words incorrectly. Part of their joke-telling skills will require them to learn how to place emphasis on certain words to achieve maximum effect.

Speech Clarity

Most students are acutely unaware of how to project their voices. This is not to say that screaming students can't cause deafness. They are simply unaware of how to *control* their voices.

What often happens when students tell jokes is that they de-emphasize important parts of the joke while mumbling information necessary for the punchline. More often than not, students are so anxious to delight friends with their witty punchlines, they blurt words out so quickly that no one hears the best part of the joke.

Exercise: *Have students tell the same joke five times. Give students feedback every time they tell the joke. Note how their delivery improves with each* *retelling, because they are less anxious about blurting out punchlines. The purpose of this exercise is to teach students how to speak clearly when they tell a joke.*

Naturalness

The best jokes are those which come naturally to us. Jokes can also feel natural if we are very familiar with them. The more we tell a joke, the more natural it will fall from our lips. The more uncomfortable we feel about telling jokes, the more awkward we appear, and the less likely it is that our listeners will relax long enough to laugh.

As you teach students how to tell jokes, encourage them to be natural. Point out to them when their speech sounds affective or fake. Teach them to use natural gestures rather than stiff movements that do not seem appropriate with the words that accompany them.

Timing

Timing is many things. It is knowing when to tell a joke, how to emphasize the right words just at the right time, and how to deliver the punchline at exactly the correct moment.

If professional comics could put timing in a jar and sell it, they would all be millionaires. Timing is probably the most difficult thing to teach or learn, but without it, your students and their jokes will never quite come across. How do you make sure they understand timing? The same way you get to Carnegie Hall: Practice, man, practice.

Establishing Rapport

Good comics establish such a rapport with audience members that people feel like they are having a personal conversation with the comic. This is true for some people to such an extent that they may respond to a comic's joke by calling out from the audience. The professional comic must then respond to the individual as the teacher needs to respond to class clowns.

Hooks

A *hook* is a cliche or popular phrase that listeners immediately recognize as funny. Rodney Dangerfield's hook is that he *"don't get no respect."* Jackie Gleason used to crack audiences up just by saying, *"how sweet it is."* Joan Rivers asks audiences, *"Can we talk?"* The purpose of a hook is to recapture an audience's attention, especially during a lull in mood. As students develop a joking style, they are likely to rely on personal "hooks" to move from one joke to another.

Save Lines

Let's face it, not every joke is going to amuse. Even the most popular comedians bomb sometimes. The difference is, professionals know to expect a poor response and they're prepared with comebacks to save the moment.

Save lines are jokes that follow a failed attempt at humor. Professional speakers use them all the time to move from a bad moment to the next part of their speech. If no one laughs, they might say, *"I just thought I'd throw that in. I guess I should have thrown it out."* If only one person laughs you might say something like, *"Thank's mom,"* or *"I don't need your pity."* Here are a few other classic save lines:

- **No, but seriously folks.**
- **Feel free to start laughing any time.**
- **Maybe I ought to speak a little slower.**
- **This next joke is for the humor impaired.**
- **I first told that joke in a biscuit factory. Everyone went crackers. (Expect a groan.)**

Going Too Far

An audience's sense of humor is not something anyone can predict until the jokes start coming. Professional comics push their audiences to the limits of their comedic endurance. No comic knows for sure what that limit is until they accidentally cross the line of tolerance.

Audience tolerance depends on the value system of audience members as well as the comedian. Don Rickles insults his savvy Catskill audiences with little protest, while another comedian trying the same jokes might be met with a hostile wall of silence. People are highly tolerant of Steve Martin and Robin Williams, allowing them more leeway than newer clowns.

Most audiences will laugh at insults about their rivals, but will not accept the same jokes if made about them. Students will learn that jokes that make classmates feel superior will be well received, while insults usually will not. The exception to this rule is the self-deprecating joke which allows classmates to laugh at the joke teller, even though he or she is a beloved member of the group.

As far as subject matter is concerned, audiences are usually tolerant of anything which is not perceived as too personal or threatening. On the one hand, jokes relieve tension about taboo or forbidden subjects. However, if a subject is too frightening, a joke will be viewed as being in bad taste and therefore unfunny. Students should avoid telling jokes about highly sensitive issues that may offend, target or victimize specific classmates or highly political issues.

One way to avoid crossing lines is to remember that all human beings have certain things in common. Most people dislike robbers, cheaters and liars, so exposing the underside of human behavior is always an acceptable subject of jokes. At the same time, most people revere human virtues. Jokes can't put down high virtues, but they can laugh at qualities that fall short of the ideal. Thus, we offend our friends if we make fun of their real moms, but most of us enjoy jokes about mothers or motherhood.

Positive Feedback

Joke telling as a dramatic exercise takes some of the fun out of a punchline. But while students understand they are not being judged based on the laughter they create, it is still demoralizing to tell a joke without getting a hilarious response.

Whether or not students are able to detach themselves from failed jokes, positive feedback is still necessary to encourage improvement. *"Criticism"* can be delivered in the form of suggestions which students can respond to. (**Example:** *"What do you think would happen if you flapped your hands when you talk about the chicken flying away?"*)

Joke-telling exercises require students to retell their jokes several times. This is necessary so that you and the other students can comment on the student's body language and make suggestions for improvement.

Another purpose of retelling the same joke many times is to reduce the impulse to laugh at one's own jokes. The inability to control one's own laughter inhibits a student's ability to control delivery and timing. By the time students are finished practicing their jokes, most will have lost the desire to laugh at themselves. In some cases, giddiness is part of a student's joke-telling style.

Teaching Joke Etiquette

In addition to learning how to tell a joke, they need to understand what is appropriate humorous subject matter, when it is polite to tell a joke, and who it is proper to tell jokes to.

Among the polite things students should learn is to be courteous when other people are telling jokes. If they have heard a joke, it is still polite to listen. Teach them not to interrupt someone who is telling a joke and not to yell out a punchline. Some students will do this because they want attention, the same way hecklers in comedy clubs are jealous of comedians on stage.

Part of any lesson on the etiquette of humor requires students to understand the difference between laughing at a clown with an exaggerated funny nose, and making fun of a real human being who actually has a big nose.

Chapter 10

THE JOY OF DRAMA

You need three things in the theatre — the play, the actors and the audience, and each must give something.

Kenneth Haigh

I. COMEDY STYLE AND TECHNIQUE

Dramatic exercises in this chapter present ideas for skits, puppet shows, and other role-playing exercises. Students can work individually, in pairs, small groups, or as a class to create comedies or mock tragedies, to express their feelings about life, and to gain experience performing in front of their peers.

121

Slapstick

Slapstick comedy is characterized by loud and boisterous farce. It is named after a paddle that was used by European actors in traveling companies. The slapstick made a funny whacking noise that delighted audiences as much as paddles in *Three Stooges* films do today.

In part, slapstick is funny because we know the victims of slapstick violence are just pretending. For a moment, we can suspend our fears of pain and laugh at people getting their fingers hammered, their ears and noses twisted or their behinds severely kicked, especially when sound effects exaggerate the impact.

Of course, there will always be a few kids who don't realize you can't really hit another human being with a hammer without getting a spanking, not even your sister who deserves it. But most kids understand the difference between funny violence and the real thing by the time they get to school. School yard bullies see to the slow learners.

Slapstick comedians are masters of timing, appearing to endure blows that would kill an elephant. A slapstick exercise could include exaggerated facial expressions and pretend violence accompanied by humorous sound effects.

Exercise: *Use the* Three Stooges *or other slapstick comedians as role models for your students. Dissect slapstick in films or videos, choosing one skit your students especially like and that is easy to perform. Divide students into groups of three stooges, each taking a role in the skit. Practice slapstick by imitating professional or classic slapstick comedians, adding sound effects from recordings available in record stores or libraries.*

Farce

Farce is a kind of ludicrous theater, full of jokes and slapstick comedy. The French and Italians elevated the farce into an artform in traveling companies during the Middle Ages and Renaissance.

The word *"farce"* comes from the French *"farcire,"* meaning to stuff, because farces were jam-packed with hilarious antics and skits. If they weren't, tomatoes, rotten vegetables and garbage let poor comedians know how the villagers felt about the show.

Parody

The word *"parody"* comes from the Greek *"paroidia,"* which was a mock-song or burlesque poem. There are actually two kinds of parody, one intentional and one accidental. Parodies imitate an author's work with the purpose of ridiculing the original, the way Aristophanes made fun of the gods in ancient Greece. Modern parodies include campy thrillers like the Rocky Horror Show, Kentucky Fried Movie, Dr. Strangelove and Mel Brooke's Frankenstein. Parody also refers to a work that is so bad that it becomes ridiculous. These are too numerous to mention here.

Exercise: *Watch a film parody and compare it with the original. Cartoons are also a good source of parody.*

Satire

Satire is the use of wit to expose folly. The word *"satire"* comes from the Latin *"satira"* which refers to a medley or mixture. Satire uses derision to point out some wickedness. The derisive laughter that comes from satirical remarks is a contemptuous laughter, often against social abuse. Among the most famous of satirists are Voltaire, Jonathan Swift, Oscar Wilde, Mark Twain and James Thurber.

Exercise: *Have students do reports on the above-named satirists, including several examples of their satirical jokes in the report.*

Irony and Wit

The word *"irony"* comes from the Greek *"eironeia,"* referring to words that convey the opposite of their literal meaning, often to produce humor. Something is ironic when it reveals some incongruity between what is expected and the way something really is. For example, Racine once said, *"it is fatal to live too long."*

Irony is considered to be the highest form of wit. It is the most difficult humor to create and is probably the best measurement of intelligence among class clowns. Students adept at irony reveal their ability to discern the complexity and nuances of life with witty, sometimes acerbic, commentaries.

Wit is defined as the ability to perceive and express, in an ingeniously humorous manner, the relationship between incongruous or disparate things. The word comes from the Old English *"weid,"* meaning *"to see."* For this reason, wit is also associated with an alert and aware mind, especially during a crisis. Thus we speak of *losing one's wits,* of being *at one's wit's end,* and of having *to keep one's wits about one.*

Irony and wit do not necessarily cause belly laughs. Sometimes when we hear something ironic, we laugh inside, or *"with tongue in cheek."*

Exercise: *Have students think of ten ironic situations, as in the following examples. Use a setup like "How come" or "Isn't it ironic. . . . "* Examples:

> Isn't it ironic that trees are most beautiful just as they lose their glorious leaves each fall?
> Isn't it funny that I never need to mail a letter when I'm near a mailbox?
> How come no one listens to you until you make a mistake?

Eirons and Alazons

Comic types are sometimes described as *"eirons"* or *"alazons."* Eirons like Woody Allen and Rodney Dangerfield are both witty self-deprecators. Eirons are usually *"straight men,"* serious people who fail because they do not understand the world around them as their listeners do. We laugh at eirons because their failures make us feel superior.

Alazons are boastful characters who pretend to be more than they are. Pedantic professors who like to pontificate are classic alazons. In the Academy Award-winning film, *The Piano,* Laurel and Hardy try to deliver a piano to a house on top of a long narrow staircase. After lugging the instrument halfway up the stairs, they encounter an alazon, a professor who wants them to step aside so he can get by. When Oliver suggests the professor should wait, the pompous prof protests, *"What! Walk around?!! Me?!!! Professor Theodore Walsh Waschenhaffel, M.D., A.D., D.D.S., F.L.D., F.F.F. and F.!"* That's an alazon.

Exercise: *Have students take on the role of eirons and alazons. As eirons, they should tell three self-deprecating jokes in a serious tone. Eirons should look wimpy and harmless, unkempt and unadjusted. Alazons exaggerate pride by puffing out their chests, lifting their heads too high, and emphasizing their importance with a too-serious expression. A sample eiron theme is that nothing seems to work.* Examples:

• Sorry I'm late but I couldn't find my glasses. Unfortunately, one of them was full.

- I can't get this match to work. It was okay when I lit it five minutes ago.
- I think I'll go into medicine. I already make my brother sick.

A sample alazon theme has the character bragging about how he or she will annihilate an enemy or a dragon. Brag until the enemy shows up, then have the alazon run away like a coward.

Commedia dell'arte

The *commedia dell'arte* originated in Italy from a long tradition of classic comedy. The Italian commedia traveled to other countries and was most popular in Europe from around 1500–1800.

The masked actors of the commedia dell'arte used improvised dialogue, satirical songs, farcical skits and pantomime to entertain their audiences. The commedia dell'arte are important because they had such a great influence on modern comedy.

Vaudeville

The word *"vaudeville"* comes from the French *chanson du Vau de Vire*, satirical songs from the Valley of Vire in Normandy.

In North America, vaudeville comedy was performed in barrooms in the late nineteenth century. Vaudeville shows were also known as "variety shows" because performers did a variety of things to entertain their demanding audiences, including magic, juggling, joke telling, dancing and singing, slapstick comedy, animal acts and impersonations.

Vaudeville acts eventually moved to the theater and then to radio and television where entertainers like Abbott and Costello performed classic bits (like *"Who's on First"*) for delighted fans. Vaudeville was a down-to-earth theater for demanding audiences. It was also a free-for-all for hopeful comics who were freely ridiculed by audiences they failed to please. George Burns once joked that when vaudeville collapsed, new talent had no place to stink.

Henny Youngman was one of the kings of vaudeville comedy. He specialized in one-liners about his wife and mother-in-law. *"My wife's so big, when she sits around the house, she sits AROUND the house,"* or *"Take my wife ... please."*

Exercise: *Assign each student three classic vaudeville "one-liners." Practice joke telling until the words flow easily and naturally. Constructive criticism* *should point out anything that takes away from the overall effectiveness of the jokes; things like "ah's" and "um's," shifting, stiffness, or, worst of all, forgetting the punchline. Here are a few classic Vaudeville one-liners to get you started.*

> I don't mean to criticize my mother's cooking, but last night she burned the ice cream.
>
> The teacher said, "You can't sleep in my class." I told her, "I could if you didn't talk so loud."
>
> A guy walks into a restaurant and says, "Waiter, do you serve crabs here?" The waiter said, "We serve anyone, sir."
>
> Then there was the guy who was crazy about Islam. I guess you could say he was a Mecca-damian nut.
>
> Know why the kid tiptoed past the medicine cabinet? He didn't want to wake up the sleeping pills.
>
> Short story—"Look here," I said to the principal. . . .
>
> As the lettuce said to the refrigerator, "Shut the door, I'm dressing."
>
> My mother's a great lady. I've known her practically all my life.

Anecdotes

Telling longer jokes is something that improves with age. Very young children have difficulty telling anecdotes because they have not yet learned how to filter out non-essential information. For the youngest students, "anecdotes" can consist of very short stories. Older students can tell longer anecdotes with more complicated setups, punchlines and ambiguity.

II. IT'S SHOW TIME!

Like many skills, students learn to perform best by doing. This section suggests performance exercises to help students improve their joke-telling skills.

Impersonations

Imitation jokes make fun of a person by exaggerating their most outstanding features. Dramatic impersonations are a good way to teach students how to create a contrast between the real or ideal world and the world of absurdity.

Exercise: *Have students pick a favorite character they would like to impersonate. As a homework assignment, they should study their character's gestures, dress, voice tone and common expressions. Isolate the character's most outstanding features. During classroom performances, see if classmates can guess who they are imitating.*

Clowning Around

Clowns offer a good example of how people can be impersonated in a humorous way. Everything about the clown is an exaggeration or an understatement. Clown clothing is either too big or too small. Noses are giant and extra red, lips cover half the face, and shoes exaggerate the size of their feet.

Exercise: *Organize a clown contest. Use stage makeup and let students create unique faces, hairstyles and costumes. Students can work in pairs or small groups to work out clownish skits.*

Pantomime

The dramatic art of pantomime was created in ancient Rome during the reign of Augustus. In the original pantomime, one actor or *"mime"* acted out all the parts of a play without uttering a word, although music and singing were performed in the background.

Pantomime was adapted by the Italian commedia dell'arte which used specific mime conventions in its farces and humorous plays. The commedia dell'arte troops traveled during the Middle Ages, taking pantomime and other humorous conventions throughout Europe.

The French Marcel Marceau (b. 1923) is the most famous mime of the modern world. Marceau performs around the world, most often as his sad-faced clown character, Bip.

Exercise: *Let students practice some common pantomime exercises as described in library books on the subject. Pretend to touch a wall, look in a mirror, or to communicate action just by the movement of their bodies and the expression on their faces.*

Improvisation

Improvisation is the spontaneous acting out of imaginary situations. Unlike play-acting with memorized lines, improvisation taps the very essence of your young student's creativity, calling for them to pretend and make-believe on many levels.

Improvisation requires students to lose their inhibitions about being in front of the class doing something silly while their peers laugh and jeer. In fact, students are intimidated by improvisation, at first. Once they see one improvised skit, most students are anxious to impress fellow classmates and their teacher with skills normally reserved for family members.

Exercise: *Divide students into groups of three. Have them improvise skits on a moment's notice by presenting them with secret roles. Skits can be relevant to the day's lesson.* Example: *(After studying the American Civil War)*

Student 1: **You are Abraham Lincoln, trying to avoid war against the South.**
Student 2: **You are from Connecticut, and against slavery.**
Student 3: **You are the owner of a Georgia cotton plantation.**

Puppet Fun

In the olden days before television, people of all ages were entertained by puppets. Throughout Europe, classic puppets corresponded to characters in the live theater, particularly those of the Italian *commedia dell'arte.*

Audience members grew to love these highly recognizable characters like the harlequin, the village constable, the nagging housewife and her disobedient children. Puppet shows were full of slapstick humor as well as moral lessons, moving easily from silliness to high drama.

The fact that young people continue to enjoy puppet shows attests to the integrity of this humorous art form. Perhaps it is because young students have a natural ability to fantasize when they see puppets, easily accepting them as real beings.

Teachers recognize the puppet as a valuable teaching tool, often allowing children to express themselves indirectly at a time in their lives when they are not yet able to communicate directly.

What is it that makes students laugh when they see puppets behaving in a silly way? In part, it is the delight students feel when adults act silly. Psychologists say silly adult puppets make children feel comfortable about laughing at grown-ups. Silly adult puppets also make students feel superior, which is what some kinds of laughter is all about.

Practically any story can be adapted to a humorous puppet script. Choosing a puppet script will depend on the personality of your students. Your script can be a story your students know and enjoy. Adapting the script may require you to change queens to kings (to accommodate a large number of boys), or to add and delete characters.

The number of characters in your play will depend on the number of students in your class. Choose characters for them who reflect the student's own personalities, or give them very different characters and see how well they play the role of someone unlike themselves.

The best way to ensure that students are enthusiastic about a puppet show is to let them participate in every phase of the show, including choosing a script they like.

Making Puppets

Making puppets teaches students about the symbolism of the theater. Yarn wigs or doll hats can show the puppet is a girl or boy or a specific profession. Use a graduation hat for the professor; a beret to create a Frenchman. Babies carry bottles; bakers carry a loaf of bread or a pie.

The simplest puppets can be made from paper lunch bags, mittens or socks. Glue on paper hair, noses, eyes and lips.

Stuff a sock full of newspaper to create a stiff stocking puppet. You can also stuff paper lunch bags with newspaper. Draw faces on the bags and attach these to rulers or sticks.

Another simple puppet consists of a paper doll attached to a tongue depressor. Small paper plates attached to tongue depressors can function as puppet faces. Colored yarn can be pasted onto these for hair.

Older students are capable of creating more complex puppet figures. Virtually any round object can function as a puppet head. Sponge or foam rubber balls, styrofoam spheres, or balls made from aluminum foil can be pierced easily with pin-on button eyes, noses and mouths. Popcycle sticks, rulers or tongue depressors can function as holders. Attach a piece of cloth to the head with safety pins to create the puppet's outfit, or use doll clothing if it is available in the right size.

A creative variation of the classic people-oriented puppet show is to make puppets of insects, dinosaurs, flowers, animals or other non-human characters. Your puppet show can be titled things like *"A Day at the Zoo"* or *"A Day on the Farm."* A play with non-human characters will be similar to human stories since your animals or insects will personify human events and emotions.

Puppet Show Time

To create a stage, place a board across a table. Drape a sheet over this where students can hide. Another type of stage is made from a large cardboard refrigerator box in which a square is cut to create the stage. The drawback to this type of stage is that only two puppeteers can fit in the box, and you risk losing your stage to the whims of gravity if students knock it over in the midst of the *denouement.*

At any rate, once you have a stage, your students are ready to perform! Students can put on a puppet show using scripts which can be read, or they can memorize their lines and *"ad lib."*

Teach students to create humorous voices for their puppets which reflect the puppet's role in the play. The nagging housewife should have a high-pitched, grating voice. The constable should have a deep, gruffy voice. Exaggerated voices are part of what makes a puppet show humorous. You must also teach students how to project their voices.

Puppet body language is one of the skills students will learn at show time. Teach students how to move their puppets; how to move up and down when they walk, to nod "yes" or shake their head "no." Students manipulate puppets with the movement of their hands and arms, which is a good way to teach them to understand how to control the movement of their characters.

Dress rehearsals help students work out the bugs in the production. Videotaping is a good way to let students see how their puppet looks to the audience. A public performance of the puppet show puts the entire dramatic production together, from the creation of costumes and characters to the creation of a complete drama that moves from beginning to middle to end.

III. SIMULATION LEARNING

Simulations allow students to learn as they role play. In a simulation exercise, students take on the role of a parliament, a jury or even rival armies to better understand the lesson. Courtroom simulations can be used to teach justice, war simulations can be used to teach history and parliament simulations that allow students to take on the roles of famous personages will help them appreciate political science.

Students love simulation learning because it is more interactive and meaningful. When lessons become personal, students care more about them. Simulation dramas are social experiences that teach students how to interact with others. This contributes to the group's sense of camaraderie and togetherness.

Try conducting a simulation exercise with another class to inject a greater element of surprise in the lesson. In cases where students simulate a historical event, they may become good enough to perform in front of the entire school.

Another advantage of simulation dramas is that they do not require a large budget for supplies. While you may be able to create costumes or props as part of a classroom project, the majority of simulations can rely more on student imagination than on expensive paraphernalia.

One way to keep a simulation exercise exciting is to withhold information from students until it is time to act out a situation. For example, in a courtroom simulation, you can continue to introduce witnesses or clues that dramatically change the situation and make the simulation less predictable.

Fashion Show Fun

Staging a fashion show teaches students to feel comfortable performing in front of their peers. Fashions can be created as part of an arts and crafts project. This exercise can appeal to both boys and girls, and to their sense of humor, by making monster, dinosaur or alien jewelry.

Celebrity Look-Alike Contest

Imitation is at the heart of all dramatic exercises. People learn by imitating others. We also laugh when we see people acting out recognizable behavior.

To stage a celebrity look-alike contest choose a theme and have students make costumes, hats or other features which allow others to recognize who they are supposed to be. Contests should have some consistent theme (such as historic characters, country music or even teachers) to give the contest a sense of continuity.

Music Videos

Music video is everywhere today. There's MTV, of course, but we also see music video in T.V. commercials for products like Nike shoes and Pepsi-Cola. Music video themes range from love and relationships to bigger issues like the plight of the homeless and the environment.

By studying music videos, students discover how to create their own videos. Begin by studying your selection of appropriate songs. Have students listen to the music and ask them to conjure images that might express the lyrics. This is a good way to reinforce their understanding of metaphors and symbolism. You can also teach music as part of the lesson, reviewing the differences between Rap, R&B, Rock n' Roll, Pop and Country music.

Another part of the lesson of music video is how this kind of creative music project is a team effort. Review for students how the song-writer, musicians, photographers, choreographers and directors all have different jobs to perform.

Divide students into groups consisting of a director, musicians and choreographer as well as judges. Students select songs from those you make available to them, usually something upbeat and socially redeeming. Choreographers then work with directors and musicians to come up with workable music video plans.

There are two ways to make music videos a fun project. Students can lip-sync to existing videos. Dances can consist of simple line dances or something more complex, depending on the age and abilities of your students.

A more complex way to make music videos is to have students create their own sets, make up their own dances, sing their own songs and play their own instruments. Break students into groups of four or five people as they work on their projects. Appoint a couple of students to act as judges and start your own video hit parade.

Chapter 11

COMPUTER FUN

Lead them by what amuses them, so that they may better discover the bent of their minds.

Plato, *The Republic*

In the olden days, we could say the dog ate our homework. Nowadays, students can tell us the cat chewed their disk. Like it or not, we're in the computer age. Even the most unyielding of traditionalists must have admitted by now that the confounded things are here to stay.

Computers, like all new technology, suffered early criticisms born of fear of change. Some worried machines would replace teachers in the classroom. Others supposed computers were self-reliant entities that could do everything but fix the kitchen sink. Nothing, of course, is further from the truth. Computers can fix sinks too.

No, but seriously folks. We all now realize that computers are not the monsters we once feared. They are simply an entertaining teaching tool, similar to books, supplementing the human element in the classroom. Even with user-friendly software, students still need the guidance of teachers to supplement their computer lessons and ruin their days.

When computers first appeared in classrooms, jokes helped to alleviate some of the tension educators felt about this new, sometimes threatening equipment.

Did you know they've made a computer that can even approach human behavior?

—Every time the computer makes a mistake it blames another computer.

Then there were those who feared that computers might isolate students, turning them into little robots. (Actually, that might not be so bad.) In reality, computers simply allow students to work at their own pace. Individualized instruction keeps students motivated as they progress, without making them feel inadequate when they do not excel at the same pace as others.

Educational psychologists tell us that computers teach hand-eye coordination, number, letter and word recognition, spatial relationships, reflexes, decision making and how to follow directions. After extensive research, top specialists have also revealed that computers are a lot of fun.

In previous chapters it was noted that children often laugh at the adult world to express anxiety about having little control over their lives. Computer-based learning is one way to give students control in the normally restrictive environment of school. When students are allowed to interact with a computer, to have some choice about what they want to learn, the classroom becomes a less forbidding place. Computers do this with color and noise and ever increasingly higher-quality graphics, making this teaching-learning thing almost fun.

I. COMPUTER TECHNOLOGY 101

Computer people use obscure words to confuse us so they can talk in private about RAM and ROM and things like integrated systems. But computer talk is like Pig Latin. Once you know a couple of rules and 12 vocabulary words, you can hang around computer nerd parties and interface for hours.

This section is for the computer uninitiated and also for those of us who are brave enough to admit new technology can be confusing. Here are a few of the basics:

Computers

Essentially, there are four kinds of computers. The smallest and simplest is the *micro-computer*. All *personal computers* are micro-computers which are small, user friendly, and affordable to individuals. Personal computers are *dedicated* to one user at a time.

The second kind of computer is the *mini-computer.* Mini-computers are typically found in small offices because they allow several users to share a system at once. *Mainframe computers,* found in many libraries, allow dozens of users to work at once. *Super computers,* capable of making hundreds of millions of calculations per second, can make predictions about distances in space, quickly redesign a complex blueprint, or determine the precise moment when your students will drive you absolutely nuts.

Computers were once too large and expensive to be practical for educational purposes. By 1979, Apple computers were being used for educational purposes. In 1981, IBM introduced the PC, their trademark for a mass market Personal Computer. IBM upgraded their PC's, first with the XT, then the AT. IBM's most recent PS/2 bears testimony to the fact that upgrades and improvements are a constant phenomena.

IBM allows other companies to produce *clones,* computers that do almost the same things the IBM name brand does. Of course, IBM was not the only company to develop a personal computer. Among the most popular computers for educators are the *Apple,* the *Macintosh* or *MAC,* to name a few. All of them operate like the IBM PC.

Computers operate at different speeds, measured in megahertz (millions of cycles per second). Intel gave brand names to the chip that does the calculations for a computer. Intel's 8088 chip, for example, operates at 4.77 megahertz. If you bought a computer several years ago, you may have a 286, which runs at 12 or 16 megahertz. A 386 runs at 33 megahertz, the 486 runs at 50 megahertz and so forth.

The main quality between chips is that the later models allow the computer to function faster. You can upgrade some computers by adding chips to its board, but if this is very expensive, you might consider buying a new computer.

Different computers differ in their abilities. See the section below on buying a computer to review questions you should ask before you choose one brand name over another.

Peripherals, Optionals and Attachments

Computers come with a *keyboard,* a *joystick* or a *mouse* that allow users to communicate with the machine. Joysticks are preferable in the early grades since they require less manual dexterity and because younger students don't yet know the alphabet.

In addition to the basics, you may want to acquire a few peripherals. Computer peripherals are like "options" in a car, in that you can hardly do without most of them. Peripherals include additional *disk drives* and *printers.* Other computer options include *music synthesizers* or *piano keyboards* which allow students to compose music or play piano. *Touch tablets* and *power pads* can be plugged into a computer's game port for computer finger painting.

Monitors

The quality of a monitor, like that of a television, depends upon its *resolution.* Resolution is measured in *pixels,* which are picture elements or light dots like snow on a television screen. The more dots per inch of screen, the higher the resolution is and the crisper the picture will be.

Nothing shows you are new to the computer club faster than not knowing what kind of monitor you have, something you'll describe with abbreviations:

MGA, or *Mono Graphics Adaptor,* is the simplest kind of monitor. This kind of monitor is virtually obsolete, is usually in black and white, amber or green, and is only capable of displaying text rather than pictures.

CGA stands for *Color Graphics Adaptor.* This monitor has a fairly low resolution and can show graphics but is limited to four colors on the screen at one time.

HGA, or *Hercules Graphics Adaptor,* enables black and white monitors to show graphics.

EGA means *Enhanced Graphics Adaptor* and is a higher-resolution monitor capable of showing 16 colors simultaneously.

VGA, *Video Graphics Adaptor,* has extremely high resolution and is able to display 256 colors.

Images on your monitor's screen are either *text* (words) or *graphics* (pictures). Sometimes, the text you see appears with symbols representing printer commands. Other programs show you exactly what the text will look like when it is printed. This is called *what-you-see-is-what-you-get* or *WYSIWYG* (pronounced wizzy-wig). In a WYSIWYG program, underlined or italicized words appear as they will on the printed page or hard copy.

Printers

Printers are usually described in terms of print quality. *Dot-matrix printers* offer economical, fast, but lower-quality printing. *Letter-quality printers* are more expensive and slower but give you typewriter-quality print.

Disk Drives

Computers have one or more *disk drives.* Disk drives are components that contain programs or data. There are usually two or three drives on the computer. The *hard disk drive* (or C drive) is a permanent part of the computer, hermetically sealed in boxes inside the frame. The *floppy disk drives* (the A drive and the B drive) are the chambers visible on the outside of your computer; the ones that accept 5¼" or 3½" floppy disks.

A more recent kind of disk drive is called *CD-ROM,* which stands for *"Compact Disk Read-Only Memory."* CD-ROM is a compact disk, similar to those used to record music albums, holding a couple billion more bytes of data than a floppy. (See Section II on "Memory" below.)

CD-ROM technology was developed because people wanted to be able to store large quantities of data, visual and otherwise, that can be stored and then easily retrieved, like the complete works of Shakespeare or the Oxford unabridged dictionary.

CD-ROM companies take pictures or slides and convert them into a computer file by laser cutting them onto a CD, a process which is still very expensive. To utilize CD-ROM you must have at least a 386 computer and a player unit which usually comes with software. To print files you can buy a color printer, or send your disk out to a color-separation printer.

Disk Operating Systems (DOS)

All computers have a *Disc Operating System (DOS),* software that tells the computer's hardware how to interact with the *programs* (instructions).

While IBM developed its personal computer, *Microsoft* developed IBM's disk operating system. DOS files, programs and commands have descriptive names (see your manual) which consist of a *root* (up to 8 characters) and an optional *extension* (up to three characters), introduced by a period. (Example: *Config.sys.*)

Microsoft's DOS comes in different *versions*. These versions are *upgraded* periodically. V1 (Version 1) was the first version. Later versions include the 3.1, 3.2, 3.3, 3.31, 4.0, 5.0 and so on. DOS upgrades usually work out bugs in previous versions. Since it is not expensive to upgrade, it is a good idea to do so as soon as a new version comes out.

Processing Chips

In addition to the computer and the DOS, personal computers need processing chips, which are the brains of the outfit. The *Central Processing Unit* (*CPU*) allows all parts of the system to communicate.

It was the CPU which formerly made computers so big, since they required many mechanical relays and vacuum tubes. Nowadays, the CPU is consolidated into tiny *integrated circuits* which are pressed into a *silicon or germanium chips* about the size of a thumbnail.

II. MEMORY

The first IBM PC was a machine without a hard drive and with limited memory. IBM later introduced the PC XT, which had a hard drive and more memory. The IBM PC AT (Advanced Technology) was faster and had even more memory.

Computers have two kinds of memory: ROM and RAM. Both RAM and ROM are part of the CPU built into the chips of your computer.

Read-Only Memory (*ROM*) is installed in the computer at the time it is assembled. ROM is a permanent part of the machine, the part of the computer's brain that tells the equipment how to interact and function.

Random Access Memory (*RAM*) is a computer's temporary memory. The RAM is the part of a computer's memory where information is stored or deleted by you.

The amount of RAM in your computer is limited. The more RAM you have, the more you are able to do since complicated programs require more RAM. RAM is like a desktop. The bigger your desk, the more papers you can grade at one sitting.

Bits and Bytes

Computers use a *binary number system* to create language and graphics. Ones and zeros (1 and 0), combined in groups of eight digits, create the *bytes* (characters) we see as letters and numbers. The individual ones and zeros of each byte are called *bits*.

Example: A = 01000001

Personal computers translate eight-digit binary codes into readable bytes using the *American Standard Code for Information Interchange (ASCII)*, pronounced (ask-key).

Your computer's hard drive contains millions to billions of bytes of data and is faster at locating, organizing and retrieving data than the floppy drives.

Computer Memory Capacity

Computer memory capacity is measured in K or *kilobytes*. 1K equals exactly 1,024 bytes (characters), or about 200 words. Most people find it easier to think of 1K as 1000 bytes. 1,024K is called a *megabyte* or *meg* if you want to sound cool. A megabyte is often thought of as a million bytes. Actually, a meg equals 1,048,576 bytes. CD–ROM memory capacity, by the way, is measured in *gigabytes* or *gigs*, representing billions of bytes.

Computer disks have limited storage capacity which is also expressed in "K." The more storage capacity or "K" your floppy has, the more stuff it can hold.

Computers with limited memory can usually be upgraded by adding more chips to the memory board inside the computer.

Memory Storage and Retrieval

Information, programs and commands which are stored in the ROM are a permanent part of your computer. When you turn your computer off, the ROM remains intact. RAM files, on the other hand, must be saved to the disk since they completely disappear as soon as your computer turns off.

There are two ways to save working files. The easiest thing to do is to save everything onto the hard drive. However, you should also save your files onto floppy disks to ensure a backup copy in case something happens to the hard drive. (See possible catastrophes below.)

III. WORKING WITH THE COMPUTER

Turning on the computer is called *booting up,* an expression derived from the saying *to pick yourself up by your own bootstraps.* If you have a hard drive, you will boot up the computer and work from the C drive (hard drive).

Other times you may want to insert a floppy disk into the A or B drive and work from a disk. When you work from floppy disks, the program instructions will appear on your monitor after the A or B drive reads the floppy. You can then use your keyboard, mouse or joystick to tell the computer what you want it to do.

The standard IBM-type keyboard includes *function keys* (F 1–10) as well as *alternate, control* and *shift keys.* Use your instruction manual to learn how to perform functions as you work.

Many programs include instructions to teach you how to move through an exercise. In some programs, small images, called *icons,* help you to remember program commands. For example, a trash can may be used as an icon to delete or throw away a file. Your skill level, and that of your students, will improve with use and familiarization with the equipment and your programs.

Shopping for a Computer

There are several factors to consider while shopping for a computer. Of course, you want equipment that is *user friendly.* Ease of use can usually be evaluated by the size of the manual that accompanies the equipment. If the manual is too heavy to lift, the computer is too complicated for personal use.

Another thing to remember is to limit your purchase to your specific needs. While it may be tempting to buy a computer that can double as an Indy-500 race car, don't be fooled into buying more equipment than you actually require. Too many people waste money buying technology they'll never use.

Murphy's Law dictates that your system will become obsolete approximately one hour after you purchase your non-refundable equipment. While it is necessary to keep abreast of the latest hardware and software, be skeptical of new fads. Even large companies can get into trouble if their equipment or programs are introduced before major problems are discovered. Don't get stuck with equipment that cannot be repaired for lack of parts or because a product has been discontinued.

Finally, do shop around. Read *Consumer Reports* and computer magazines to discover what the experts think about the pros and cons of the equipment you intend to buy. You should also ask friends who actively use computers what they like and dislike about the systems they have.

As you prepare to buy, make a list of everything you would like your computer to do. Then visit a computer show where you can ask hard questions of many different companies. Here are a few things to ask:

- *What kind of software programs are available?*
- *Is the computer user friendly?*
- *Is the manual easy to read? I mean really easy!*
- *Is the computer portable? Or does it come with back injury insurance?*
- *How much memory does it have? Is the memory upgradable?*
- *Is the keyboard easy for children to use? Is it detachable? Are the keys easy to press?*
- *What kind of monitor is used? What are the quality of the graphics?*
- *How many hours can you expect the computer to last in the average classroom? (That's called "Mean Time Between Failure" or MTBF.)*
- *What does the maintenance agreement entail?*
- *What kind of technical assistance does the company have? If you get in trouble, do they have an 800-number where you can scream for help?*
- *Oh, yes. How much does the computer cost? And how expensive is the software?*

Computer Maintenance in the Classroom

Once you have selected the computer that's right for you, there are a few things to remember about their use in the classroom. First, a few tips on computer care. Remember to set up the computer in a safe place—on a sturdy table and in a place where you can observe it to protect against accidents, curiosity and vandalism. Classroom computers should be placed in a traffic-free area, or even in a separate room which can be locked.

Place your computer(s) in a well-lit place, but away from direct sunlight. Computers should be kept away from excessive heat, cold or moisture that might come in through open windows. Use a surge protector and plug the computer into grounded outlets. The best outlet is one that is free of other major appliances.

Computers need to be placed away from magnets, televisions, radios or sources of static electricity, including metal objects and telephones. It is also a good idea to buy an *anti-static strip* for your keyboard to protect against static electricity generated from carpets, especially during the winter months. If static electricity is really a problem in your room, a humidifier or *anti-static rug spray* will lessen the potential damage to your computer.

Computer exercises should be limited to one hour for several reasons. Like any school activity, students grow restless when they must do the same thing for too long. Computer lessons require students to sit for a period of time, and they need to exercise when they are finished. Additionally, working with video monitors can tire the eyes.

Teachers, like students, sometimes have to learn lessons on the computer (like how to turn the thing on). Like all equipment, things can and do go wrong in class. If your computer doesn't work, check that the brightness of the monitor has been turned up. Teachers must also deal with relinquishing some control over the computers, allowing students to experiment and to make mistakes.

As with any classroom activity, instruct your students about proper computer behavior. Food and drink must never be allowed near computer equipment, nor should students carry anything (like plants or ant farms) near computers to avoid major mishaps. If students work on the computers after lunch, have them wash the cheese doodles from their hands and faces first.

Students will be anxious to touch the computers. During the first lessons, some will want to jump ahead of your instructions. This is a good sign that the computers are going to be as entertaining as you want them to be. Still, you must teach students who want to do everything by themselves that they need to follow these basic rules:

- *Keep disk drives closed when the computer is off.*
- *Keep disk drives closed when a disk is being read in the drive.*
- *Remove disks from the drive before turning off the computer.*
- *Keep the computer clean by using a dust cover after use.*
- *Have fun with the computer, but don't horseplay near the equipment. Save that for the playground, or lose computer privileges.*

What Can Go Wrong?

Here are some of the unanticipated surprises that cause some teachers to consider throwing their computer over the first available cliff:

- *Your computer can shut off momentarily, causing all unsaved working files to disappear. This can occur when there's a power surge during an electric storm, or when your electricity shuts off accidentally. Standard procedure in this case is to sit and stare at the screen for approximately ten minutes, hoping there has been some kind of mistake. To avoid losing files, save your work often. To avoid computer damage from power surges (power that goes way down then suddenly up) or power "spikes" (power pops), use a surge protector.*
- *Your computer's hard drive can contract a "virus," taking all your work to that great storage facility in the sky. You can avoid a virus by not sharing software.*
- *Your hard drive can "crash." This is similar to a scratch on a phonograph record. The normal human reaction in this case is to stare at your screen for approximately 30 minutes, praying this is just a schoolroom prank. To make sure you don't lose your work forever, save your files on floppy disks at the end of **every** work session.*
- *Your computer may not work. It won't boot up, it won't do anything. It just sits there. When this occurs, plug it in.*

IV. COMPUTER PROGRAMS

Computer programs are instructions. Programs use various computer languages which can be simple and direct or complicated and coded. One of the most common computer languages is called *BASIC*. Other familiar languages include *Pascal, Fortran* and *Turbo C*.

Computer programs are stored both on the hard drive and on floppy diskettes. *Floppy disks* are thin, circular plates which are covered with magnetized iron oxide similar to videotape and audiotape. The disk is enclosed in a square envelope to protect it from dust and peanut butter.

Software, Hardware and Firmware

Salespeople sometimes compare software to a record album and hardware to a record player. Essentially, your software, whether installed on the hard drive or on a floppy diskette, tells your computer what to do.

Software diskettes are either *single-sided* or *double-sided*. Double-sided disks are able to store more information because they use both sides of the disk, just as a phonograph record plays twice as much music when both sides are recorded.

Computer diskettes are also described according to their *density*. High-density disks can hold more information than low-density disks.

In addition to software and hardware there is *firmware*. Firmware is something between software and hardware in that it is a hard cartridge (like an Atari game) that contains software, or a computer chip with embedded instructions.

IMPORTANT: *Since many software programs only work with the hardware it was designed to serve, you need to decide in advance which company or companies can best serve your classroom needs.*

Educational Software Programs

There are several kinds of educational software, also known as *Computer-Assisted Instruction (CAI) programs.*

Drill and Practice Software reviews lessons and drills students to improve their knowledge of the material. This is the most traditional kind of educational software and is sometimes criticized as being too boring. Some programs offset such criticism with humorous interjections which encourage students as they progress through the drill. On the positive side, they offer immediate feedback on right and wrong answers, colorful displays and sometimes game formats.

What cannot be criticized is the practical nature of drill and practice software. It is particularly helpful for lessons in language learning including vocabulary, spelling and foreign languages where memorization is important. Drill and practice programs are also helpful for memorizing multiplication tables.

Creative Software helps students discover the artist within by letting them compose music, paint pictures or write poetry.

Then, of course, there are *video games*, many of them arcade style. Video games once meant little beeping dots on a screen. The really complex programs let a big dot eat other dots. Then, someone realized that virtually every kind of software can be programmed to be an interactive game. Maybe that's why there are more games than any other kind of educational program.

There are also more improvements and advances in computer games from one year to the next. Computer game production is a highly competitive and lucrative area of computer programs. Game programs teach lessons using rules, challenges, and scorekeeping to motivate as well as amuse students as they learn. I still like *Donkey Kong* the best.

If the purpose of your software is to bonk Buster on the bean, you've got a video game, not an educational program. Educational games, unlike video games, should teach more than manual dexterity. This is not to say video games are all bad. Experts note they can relieve stress, provide escape, and teach logistics. They allow students to enter the world of fantasy and require them to concentrate on problem-solving tasks. Video games also tend to be more violent and even bizarre, just like some of our classrooms.

Whatever the virtues of arcade-style video games, propriety dictates that certain games, however challenging that may be, are not appropriate for the classroom. The names of video games inappropriate for the classroom are descriptive enough not to be confused with Computer-Assisted Instruction programs.

Simulation Programs use 3-D graphics that allow students to experience places and activities outside the classroom including outer space and foreign lands. (Of course, affordable simulation programs are relatively simplistic; at least 2-dimensional, although some are 3-D.) True simulation equipment, such as that used by NASA to train astronauts, is able to recreate reality in all dimensions (sight, sound, motion and touch). Your students must use their imaginations to approximate a simulation exercise such as that provided by *Microbe,* a program that allows them to discover the human circulatory system.

Tutorial Programs introduce students to new material. The oldest tutoring program is TUTOR, introduced in 1967 as part of the University of Illinois's PLATO education system. TUTOR offers a number of different programs to meet the needs of different student capabilities.

In addition to educational software, there are general programs that can be used in the classroom. *Word processing programs* are typewriters that can edit. *WordStar, Word Perfect* and *Microsoft Word* are all popular word processing programs. *Spreadsheets* are financial programs capable of calculating and making mathematical projections. *Databases* are programs that store, sort and retrieve information, much like a hi-tech card catalog. *Desktop publishing programs* like *PageMaker* allow you to typeset newsletters and reports.

Finally, *Utilities* programs are like tools, providing computer maintenance and performance of utilitarian jobs. A *compression program*, for example, consolidates all stored information into one area to make information storage and retrieval more efficient. *Quick-DOS* is a utility which allows you to move files from one drive to another quickly and easily.

Multi-Media

Multi-media is a term that refers to computerized presentations. Let's say you're doing a search on Beethoven and you have a multi-media computer terminal. A picture will appear (moving or still) as if you're looking at a dynamic picture in a book. You can also hear in rich, CD-quality sound. Among other things, your students can look at musical notes while they are playing. The technology currently exists for multi-media presentations, but they are still not widely used.

Virtual Reality

In futuristic movies, students assimilate information in a state of *"virtual reality,"* a three-dimensional computer-generated recreation or simulation of an event. In *Star Trek: The Next Generation,* for example, people can visit the *"holodeck"* where a personalized program places them in settings that can be anything from relaxing to life-threatening. Virtual reality as a teaching tool, while still not widely used, is also not so far from general use. As with many new devices (including high-resolution TV), the technology is there, but the prices are still out of this world.

Virtual reality differs from other computer systems because it places humans rather than machines at the center of activity. Eye masks, gloves and earphones literally fit around the human body so that the computer-generated experience is interactive. Today, many fear virtual reality in much the same way we once feared the potential dangers of standard computer technology. We fear that technology will replace humans, or that technology will take over and create robots. Nothing could be further from the truth. In fact, within the next two decades, virtual reality is likely to be as cost effective and normal in the classroom as computers are now.

Virtual-reality experiences tap the whole learning process by stimulating sight, hearing, feeling and recognition, much the same way we learn in "experiential" situations like mountain climbing or swimming. Virtual reality allows us to learn by doing, without actually going anywhere. Imagine teaching a lesson about Sir Edmund Hillary's climb up Mount Everest by accompanying him on the journey! With virtual reality, students will one day be able to visualize any situation, manipulate a circumstance, and interact with computers using visual information. Instead of screens and keyboards, they will wear display masks over their eyes, headphones over their ears, and gloves on their hands. Is it possible that one of the problems teachers may face in the future is convincing students to leave the school grounds?

Shopping for Software

As with hardware, there are basic questions to ask about computer software before you spend the cash. Here are a few things to remember:

- *Will the software work on your equipment?*
- *Is the program designed for the age group you teach?*
- *Is the program interesting? Does it engage youngsters with quality graphics and challenging demands?*
- *Does the program anticipate the errors your students will make? Does the program help students find the correct answer, or just tell them they're wrong?*
- *Does the program give your students some degree of control over the direction of the lesson?*
- *What does the software cost, and is the investment worth the amount of time you'll spend using the program?*

Selected Fun Software

There are virtually thousands of companies that produce computer software. For your convenience, I have listed a few of the most popular and entertaining educational software programs currently available. Most are compatible with the most common educational computers (Apple, IBM PC, etc.). Addresses of software companies follow this section.

Alphabet Beasts & Co. (Software Productions) is an introduction to letter and number recognition.

Archon (Electronic Arts) is an adventure game in which good fights evil in a fantasy land of sorcerers, goblins, trolls and wizards.

Bank Street Writer (Broderbund Software) is a user-friendly word processing program.

Better View a Zoo (Sunburst) is a pre-reading program in which students search for wild animals in the jungle.

Cartooners (Electronic Arts) is designed to stimulate creative story-telling in a playful environment.

Dueling Digits (Broderbund Software) is a math program that includes game drills.

The Enchanted Forest (Sunburst) is a program to help students develop visualization skills, logic and observation skills.

The Factory (Sunburst) is a strategy game in which students make factory goods.

Home Word (Sierra On-Line) is a word processing program that can be used with televisions.

Kids' Corner programs (C & C Software) includes Letters and First Words and quiz programs.

Learning About Numbers (C & C Software) teaches number concepts including time and counting.

Letterman (Behavioral Engineering) is a typing program in a game format.

Letters and First Words (C & C Software) consists of three programs which help children learn to identify letters, recognize associated sounds, and to spell simple words.

Magic Crayon (C & C Software) is a drawing program.

Magic Slates (Sunburst) is entertaining reading and writing programs.

Melody Maker (Scholastic Wizware) is a music program that allows students to compose.

Micro Mother Goose (Software Productions) is a popular reading program using nursery rhymes. It includes animated illustrations and music, offered at various skill levels.

M-ss-ng L-nks: A Game of Language and Letters (Sunburst) is a game program in which students fill in the blanks of famous passages.

Playing with Science (Sunburst) is an entertaining science program.

The Pond (Sunburst) is a strategy game using frogs to hop across lily pads.

Puppet Plays (Sunburst) allow students to put on computerized puppet shows.

Ready, Set (Sunburst) is an introduction to shape and letter recognition.

Schoolhouse I (Compu-Tations, Inc.) includes Hangman, Word Fun, States and Capitols, Learn A Poem and Spelling.

Soccer Math (Compu-Tations, Inc.) is a math program in a game format for two players.

Stickybear ABC (Xerox Education) is an introduction to letter recognition.

Stickybear Numbers (Xerox Education) is an introduction to number recognition.

Story Builder (Random House) teaches young students to develop stories.

Story Starter (Random House) teaches students to create stories, available at various skill levels.

Turtle Tracks (Scholastic Wizware) is an art program using a turtle.

Type Attack (Sirius Software) is a typing program in a game format.

Typing Tutor III (Simon and Schuster) is an entertaining typing program.

Teasers by Tobbs (Sunburst) is a puzzles and problem-solving program.

In addition to the programs listed above, software called "shareware" and "public domain" offers a tremendous opportunity for low-cost or free programs. These are available from local computer clubs or from national distributors. Your local library may also have its own program library available for you to copy. Addresses for several shareware companies are listed below.

Software Manufacturers

Behavioral Engineering, 230 Mt. Hermon Rd., Scotts Valley, CA 95066.

Broderbund Software, 500 Redwood Blvd., Novato, CA 94901; (415) 382-4600.

C & C Software, 5713 Kentford Circle, Wichita, KS 67220; (800) 752-2086; (316) 683-6056.

Compu-Tations, Inc., 24361 Greenfield Rd., #103, Southfield, MI 48075-3162; (800) 345-2964; (313) 557-9280.

Electronic Arts, P.O. Box 7530, San Mateo, CA 94403; (415) 571-7171.

Milliken Pub. Co., 1100 Research Blvd., St. Louis, MO 63132; (314) 991-4220; (800) 643-0008 or (800) 325-4136. (*Entertaining educational software available in a variety of subject areas including reading, writing,* *language arts, mathematics, problem solving, science, children's literature, and skill builders.*)

Random House School Division, 400 Hahn Rd., Westminster, MD 21157; (800) 733-3000.

Scholastic Wizware, 1290 Wall St. West, Lyndhurst, NJ 07071.

Sierra On-Line Inc., Sierra On-Line Building, P.O. Box 485, Coarsegold, CA 93614. (209) 683-8989. (*Offers educational, interactive, and mind-stimulating computer games including music programs and adventure games.*)

Simon and Schuster, 1230 Ave. of the Americas, New York, NY 10020.

Sirius Software, 10364 Rockingham Dr., Sacramento, CA 95827.

Software Productions Inc., 2357 Southway Dr., Columbus, OH 43221.

Sunburst Computer Courseware, Rm. B7 39 Washington Ave., Pleasant-ville, NY 10570; (800) 628-8897; (914) 747-3310 (call collect).

Xerox Education Publications, 245 Long Hill Rd., Middletown, CT 06457.

Public Domain Software Companies

AccuSoft Public Domain & Shareware, 14761 Pearl Rd., Suite 309, P.O. Box 360888, Strongsville, OH 44136; (800) 487-2148.

Public Brand Software, P.O. Box 51315, Indianapolis, IN 46251; (800) 426-3475.

Reasonable Solutions, 2101 West Main St., Medford, OR 97501; (800) 876-3475.

Software International Exchange, 6540 W. Atlantic Blvd., Margate, FL 33063; in Florida call (305) 970-4366; out of state, call (800) 950-4366. Tech support is available.

Chapter 12

ENVIRONMENTAL FUN

To-morrow I'll reform, the fool does say;
To-day itself's too late — The wise did yesterday.

Benjamin Franklin, *Poor Richard's Almanac*

"DON'T THINK OF IT AS *PLAGIARISM*, MRS.
KEPLAR, THINK OF IT AS *RECYCLING!*"

When I was just a tot, fun in the classroom was usually associated with rewards for good behavior. If we were "good" (which generally meant "quiet"), we received extra time at recess or we were allowed to play a special game. Nowadays, fun at school is more often connected with the real world; a world that is introduced to children at a younger age with serious issues like AIDS, sexual abuse and the future health of our planet taking an increasingly important place next to the liberal arts.

This chapter is about how the classroom has changed since I was a youngster as our world has become more environmentally aware. It is also about how teachers can adapt to the needs of today's classroom, where environmental awareness is more important than ever before.

What's So Funny About the Environment?

There is much irony in environmental humor, and environmental jokes have much in common with crisis humor, sick jokes and gallows humor. For example:

> George: Guess what! My book on the inevitable destruction of the earth just got accepted by a big New York publisher.
>   Mary: Yeah, but who's going to read it?

Here's another example of that same quality:

> A man was in court for killing a rare white tiger. The judge asked why he did it. "Your honor," the man said, "I was lost in the jungle. I hadn't eaten for days. Killing that white tiger was all I could do to survive."
> The judge thought a moment then said, "Your charges are dismissed. I can't sentence you for trying to stay alive. But tell me, what does a white tiger taste like?"
> The man scratched his chin. "Oh, I don't know," he said. "Sort of a cross between gorilla and bald eagle."

Logically, environmental jokes are similar to "sick" jokes because they function in much the same way . . . to make us feel comfortable about an unfunny subject, and to relieve anxiety about it. In fact, many environmental jokes are associated with environmental crisis like the Alaskan oil spill from the *Exxon Valdez* or the nuclear disasters at Three Mile Island and Chernobyl.

> Did you see Marc's socks? They were so bright, the wool must have come from Chernobyl sheep.

Environmental jokes associated with our planet focus attention on issues like nuclear power which we fear in a similar way that gallows humor focuses on fears associated with death. For example:

> Does it scare you that France has nuclear weapons? What would make them want to use the bomb? Maybe when Ernest and Giulio Gallo win one too many wine contests.

Other earth-conscious jokes serve to make us more aware of animal rights or endangered species:

> I feel sorry for chinchillas, don't you? How would you like to find out you were raised to be a coat?

Jokes that qualify as "environmental" jokes are not only about climate, wildlife and nature. Nowadays, people have a "whole earth" approach to the planet which encompasses anything that effects either the health of the planet or the health of the people, plants and animals who depend on the earth for their survival and existence.

One of the most popular categories of pseudo-environmental jokes makes fun of health foods, something which has become popular with greater awareness of the hazards of pesticides and preservatives. Scatological jokes concentrate on the power of grains, while another category of jokes focuses on how tasteless food can be when it has no fat, sugar or nitrates for flavor.

> Have you heard of tofu? Who invented this anyway? It's the only food I know that's colorless, odorless *and* tasteless. What a concept. Isn't that a little like changing the wine into water?

> And who invented yogurt? I mean, how can you tell when it's bad? What did someone say one day, "Let it sit on the counter for a month, then we'll eat it."

Like crisis humor, health jokes relieve anxiety about the difficulties of dieting and the rigors of a healthy life-style. Unlike the 1960s when drug and alcohol-related jokes were accepted by adolescents as "cool," "just say no" campaigns, celebrity advertisements against drugs, as well as the hard-luck confessions of so many successful Americans has brought a new negative stigma to the subject of drugs. Now we ask, *"Why do you think they call it dope?"* In standup comedy clubs, audiences still laugh at comedians who pretend to be stoned, but not because they can relate. They're laughing because most of us think people who take drugs are stupid.

Another group of health-related food jokes pokes fun at "junk food." This kind of joke serves as a social criticism of lower standards in food we may enjoy, even while we know it is not good for us to eat. All the fast-food chains are targets for health food jokes, and so are many brand-name foods whose popularity may have waned as American consumers search for high-grain, low-fat substitutes.

> Did you know that ants don't recognize Wonder Bread as a food source? I don't know about you, but I don't want to put anything in my mouth that's a better bug repellant than Raid.

> My roommate wasn't exactly a health food nut. Let's just say he thought Twinkies were a legitimate food group.

Environmental food jokes also criticize abuses associated with the production of food, in some cases adapting old jokes to new problems:

Waiter, there's a fly in my soup.
That's okay, we won't charge you extra.

Hey, there's dolphin in this tuna.
That's okay, we won't charge you extra.

Similarly, as people become more sensitive to the issue of second-hand smoke, with many airline flights and public buildings becoming smoke-free, socially conscious jokes making fun of smokers put pressure on people to quit. Such jokes name names and therefore put pressure on the corporations who produce products that could be harmful.

Have you heard Camel cigarettes' jingle, "I'd walk a mile for a camel." Well if you've been smoking for ten years, I guarantee you're not going to jog for one.

Environmental Games We Should Play

Our earth is made up of a *finite* amount of four elements: earth, wind, fire and water. Respecting each of these elements and teaching respect for them is one of the most important lessons you can teach in your classrooms.

Environmental lessons can be integrated into any of the playful activities suggested in this book, from joke telling to puzzle making, from games you play to dramas or talent shows you present in the course of your regular curriculum.

Fortunately, children are naturally curious about our planet. And why not? It's all new to them. Every stone, every leaf, every soft grassy meadow represents something which can be associated with fun. Still, it is the teacher who must teach students to "stop and smell the roses" while we still have roses to smell.

Teachers can open young eyes to the natural world by taking every opportunity to openly discuss issues like acid rain, global warming, the burning of the rain forests, the plight of endangered animal or plant species or the depletion of the ozone layer. Fun exercises are the best way to make sure students have positive associations with the earth they will inherit as adults.

Field Trips: Fun in Your Own Back Yard

There's good news about the new environmental curriculum . . . it doesn't have to cost a thing. No textbooks are required. No major investment is needed. Everything you could possibly want to show your students is right in your own back yard.

Field trips to the natural world, unlike trips to science museums or factories, offer a chance to integrate the field trip with the classroom, because you can bring a bit of the earth back into your classroom on an ongoing basis. In the spirit of recycling, your students will learn ultimately to give back to the planet everything they borrow.

Field trips to the natural world can include the following, although your imagination is truly the limit of what you do and where you go:

Take a field trip to the woods. Your field trip will have two purposes: (1) to make your students more conscious of not disturbing the environment by sticking to paths, and by looking without touching and (2) to learn the basics of the natural world with subjects like ecosystems, seasonal changes, and games to see who can find or name the most plants or animals.

Take a trip to a tree farm. Tree farms grow trees specifically for use. Trees in uniform rows may be destined to become Christmas trees or to be replanted to replace timber farms. Showing students this kind of responsible tree care is a good forum to discuss controversial subjects like burning rain forests or the timber industry. Debates and simulation dramas, staged in a fun way, will allow your students to explore different sides of issues rather than to simplify various points of view as "good" or "bad," "right" or "wrong." Students, dressed as lumberjacks or as farmers, for example, can still have fun while learning to think about serious issues for themselves, including the short-term and long-term consequences of the human use of the earth's plant and animal life.

Take a trip to a plant store. Have the employee working in the plant store explain different kinds of plants, about pot sizes, cuttings and replantings, what fertilizers do and so forth. Let your students adopt a plant that can endure the environment of the classroom and use it for lessons year round. Plants that are capable of being replanted in smaller pots teach the best lessons of conservation and recycling. When possible, students can replant the cuttings from their adopted parent plant in a natural setting.

Take a field trip to a fish hatchery. Fish farms are another unique way to educate students about the responsible use of wildlife. We can't all be vegetarians, after all. But we can support efforts to repopulate streams, lakes and rivers. Environmental lessons should be about giving back if we borrow from nature so there are plenty of resources for generations to come.

Fun with Our Changing Seasons

The changing seasons, like holidays, present a perfect opportunity to combine fun and games with valuable lessons about respecting our earth.

Fortunately, the school year begins after a summer break at one of the most beautiful seasons of the year. Fall is a time when the changing of the season is most visible. It is therefore the most appropriate season in which to set the stage for your classroom's high sensitivity to the importance seasonal changes have in their lives.

Assuming your classroom has trees near your school, have your class adopt one of them and periodically visit it to see how it is changing over the months. If your school is located in an urban environment, bring a perennial plant into your room, and schedule special lessons around bloom and remission times. Cactus which bloom periodically are easy to care for and can usually survive the classroom environment with its air conditioning, heat and sometimes less-than-optimal lighting. Advice from your local plant store will allow you to either bring seasonal plants (like poinsettias) to your room periodically or as a permanent part of your room.

One of the most important lessons of the changing season relates to the importance of conservation. While it is tempting in our world of excesses to throw away "trash," students can learn that nothing in the natural is ever wasted. This basic lesson has much broader implications because it not only affects the student's everyday life in school. Additionally, your students will become spokespersons in the home for a sometimes less aware generation.

Here are some activities which can take advantage of the seasons to teach conservation and recycling on a daily basis:

Set up a recycling system in your room. Paper is divided into white and colored sheets. Cans and bottles can be turned in to a recycling center periodically for cash to be used to fund the recycling program. When someone has something which appears to be "trash" and they can't figure out what to do with it, have a class discussion and come up with ideas about what you might do with, say, an empty orange juice can or toilet paper roll. Many such items can be used for craft projects which have environmental themes.

Build a compost pile. Compost is a mixture of decaying organic materials which acts as a natural fertilizer. In nature, leaves that fall from trees decay naturally at the base of the tree. In your classroom, you will have to find organic materials which can be turned in a dirt pile, then used as fertilizer to plant a flower or vegetable garden in the spring. Books on composting are widely available in bookstores and libraries. You can also contact your local environmental agencies to come to your school to talk about government regulations and the science of composting. Build your compost pile in the classroom (they can be purchased at a hardware store) or find a spot outside where the pile will be safe from animals.

Have a "fix it" day. Have students bring in small objects from home that are broken. Over time you will have a box full of wheels, doll heads, plastic chips and so forth. Students can use their imagination to create something new from something discarded. As a recycling challenge, have them try to create a new item which can be used as a true example of "recycled." For example, make plant holders out of a discarded toy truck.

Make seasonal bulletin boards. These can teach students about what plants are most typical for the time. This can also be a lesson on why summer fruits are either more expensive or unavailable in December. Extend this to a weather and geography lesson to explain how oranges come from the Southern Hemisphere (like Brazil) in December when it is summer there and winter here. Or a lesson in high-tech farming, as in the way Israel grows bananas year round in spite of its desert climate.

Appreciating the Animal World

With the exception of domestic pets, many children never have the opportunity to see real live animals up close. Two obvious places to visit animals are the local zoo or a farm. Many zoos have petting areas where children can safely touch younger animals like sheep and pigs. Petting pools in science museums, aquariums or public zoos bring children closer to underwater creatures like starfish, mollusks and coral.

The importance of making positive, real associations with living animals while children are still young cannot be overestimated. In some cases, children can be cruel to animals, throwing trash or food into a zoo animal's cage, for example, to try to catch its attention. The only way to sensitize children to the animal world is to bridge the gap between the fantasy, storybook world most children have with animals, and the real world of wonderful, but limited living creatures.

One good way to sensitize students to animals is to adopt a pet in your classroom. The obvious difficulty here is that you, the teacher, will end up doing any extra work (during holidays and on summer vacation, for example) that needs to be done. Cleaning cages, feeding and petting, however, are all activities that can belong to the students themselves. Setting up a rotating schedule teaches leadership, responsibility, and gives everyone a fair chance to be a pet owner for a short while.

A valuable lesson for today's youngsters is also associated with animal cruelty and responsible pet care. Visit your local humane society or a local vet for a good, fun lesson on proper animal maintenance. Students can be made aware, in a sensitive way, about the problem of euthanasia which has become necessary in so many humane societies because people simply didn't spay or neuter their pets.

Endangered species is an especially important subject and one that can be taught in a humorous way. Your students can each adopt one endangered species, for example, using it in their artwork, in cartoons or jokes they create, or as a subject of a crossword puzzle in which all clues are related to their animal. They can also make a costume to represent their animal while reading a report to educate the other students about where the animal is found, who its predators are, and what can be done to save it. As an additional exercise, students can adopt one of the many beautiful but completely extinct species, including the carrier pigeon, and teach each other about animals we humans can no longer enjoy.

Another way to personalize the plight of endangered animals is to create a futuristic world for your students. Have them imagine what the world will be like in 100 years. They can describe their endangered species, draw pictures for future generations with personal letters to future children their own age, describing what the world around them is like. Then plant your letters and pictures in a time capsule so students can feel they have made friends with a future generation in a concrete way.

Organic Cooking, New Lessons in Home Economics

With a growing awareness of the dangers of pesticides and preservatives, organic farming and cooking is becoming more popular. At the very least, your students should have lessons on how to choose natural foods, how to read grocery store labels and how to prepare foods naturally, and all of this can be highly entertaining. If you ever saw my 16-grain loaf of bread ($3/4''$ high) you would know what I mean.

Baking bread is a fun lesson because it utilizes the most basic recipe on earth to create a seemingly magical, usually tasty treat. Your basic ingredients, bread flour, yeast, water or milk and seasonings, form the basis of every kind of bread you or your students can possibly imagine, and they will imagine them all. Lessons associated with bread can include an introduction to preservatives, since bread without them has a rather short shelf life. In fact, watching bread with and without preservatives is a good lesson on the pros and cons of chemicals.

Pumpkins are perfect for lessons on recycling because the pumpkin meat can be used for a pie, the cask for a lantern, the seeds for snacks, and the remaining gook for a compost pile. Here students learn to maximize food rather than to waste it. A lesson can follow on cultures like the Chinese who use every bit of land for growing food, and eat every edible part of plants and animals in order to feed a billion people. There are many cultural lessons students will find funny, like the way some Arabs consider sheep eyeballs to be a delicacy. Challenge students by having them think about how to maximize food we normally throw into the garbage disposal like carrot tops or onion skins.

Another easy food lesson can revolve around the apple. Apples are easy to bake and can be made into so many different things. You can even mash them up and throw them into some bread recipes. Apple sauce, apple pie, baked apples, ambrosia salad are just a few of the ways to teach students that many foods have multiple uses, with "garbage" better served as bird food or compost matter than simply throwing it away.

Whole Earth Handicrafts: Making History Come Alive

Once your students discover the natural world, it will be just a matter of time before organic materials begin making their way into your classroom, either for temporary display or so that discarded material can be put to good use.

In many cases, America's early ancestors had to rely on organic materials to create the only toys and holiday decorations they had to enjoy. Christmas trees, for example, were strung with popcorn or with kernels of corn, dried peas or beans or colorful cranberries organized in an interesting design. Your students will not only have fun while they decorate the room, they will learn valuable lessons about recycling and conservation from a historical generation that used to rely on such practices as a matter of course.

In some cases, the lessons you are trying to teach may seem hypocritical. While you teach your students to respect the forest, to a certain extent, you have to pillage the forest for nuts and pine cones for some of your lessons. This, too, is a lesson for your students; teach them that conservation is about being "conservative" in the use of supplies. Excesses, waste without reason and neglect are the enemies of our earth and our species. You must also teach individual responsibility since each person must understand the overall impact of their little actions over time.

Environmental Fun with Local Experts

One of the best ways to entertain your students while secretly teaching them high-impact environmental lessons is to invite interesting local experts to your classroom. While there are good speakers who occasionally visit your school (like a visit from a police or fire professional), consider inviting some non-traditional speakers to make a personal appearance in your classroom.

Consider, for example, inviting your local television weather personality to explain (in simple terms) how the weather is affecting our earth. Weather forecasters on television are trained to speak in front of cameras, and they are often entertaining speakers. Many television stations offer tours of the studio. If you arrange it in advance, you might convince your local weather person to let the students predict their own weather so they can see themselves on TV. If you are lucky enough to have a science museum in your area, they may also have a weather wall for this purpose.

Another non-traditional speaker is a naturalist, either from a local park, from the Audubon society, zoo or local nature club. While people from nature groups may not speak on a regular basis, they can often be relied upon to bring animals or wildlife to your classroom. As with a television personality, you can heighten the experience of a speaker by having them come to the classroom prior to a field trip to a natural setting.

Additionally, an ongoing class project will heighten any learning experience associated with a field trip. For example, in a lesson about endangered species, your class can raise animals (fish are easy), then release them in the wild. In a lesson on ecosystems, the students can grow a plant, then replant it in a correct environment.

For practical reasons, great speakers on the lecture circuit address entire schools at a time. This means there is less chance for personal interaction and individual questions from the students. As often as possible, do make your visiting expert a close encounter for your students. Limit the visit to your classroom, and have the students write a thank-you note after the visit including something they learned about the environment from the guest.

Again, seek non-traditional local experts for the most unique speakers. Contact your local Chamber of Commerce for a list of local clubs, or tap the expertise of your students' parents. Invite someone in from a local recycling plant, from your state's government office, or from a corporation so your students can hear different perspectives on why industry, management and government operate the way they do. Once students understand how different groups feel about an issue, you are then in a position to create fun games, simulations, debates or competitions related to environmental topics.

Environmental Safety in the Classroom

Among the inroads American schools have made in the past two decades is a greater awareness of potential hazards in the classroom. Legislation passed which required schools to remove asbestos, once widely used as a building material, is an example of more responsible, aware actions. Not that problems like asbestos and lead paint were immediately remedied. It simply cost too much to be solved quickly. You know the saying, "We want the very *best* for our children . . . *as long as it doesn't cost anything.*"

This is not to imply negligence. So many environmental hazards went unnoticed because we had no idea they existed. Radon is one example of this. However, it must be noted that more environmental groups are educating the general public about potential hazards, and more ordinary citizens are actively dealing with real situations. In the classroom, teachers can and should take an active role in making sure that supplies like clay, glue and even cleaning materials are not toxic.

Teachers can go a step further and seek out recycled supplies, or complain about excessive packaging or the use of some packing chips and other non-biodegradable materials. Teach your students that sometimes "less *is* more," but when it comes to packaging, "more is usually less." Buying in quantity just makes "cents."

The Importance of Fun in the Natural World

Every generation looks at the next generation with a mixture of nostalgia and horror. "When I was a youngster" has been a cliche since the first cave parents criticized their children for planting gardens instead of relying on mammoths for their next meal. Somewhere in time, we humans stopped thinking about having enough and started thinking about having more than enough.

Throughout history, luxury has been associated with excess. Big cars and giant houses have long been part of the American Dream. In the past two decades all that has changed. Since the gas crisis, most of us think of big cars as "gas guzzlers." Droughts around the country have made Americans more conscious of water conservation. And the recession has made it necessary for many American families to go from one-income households to two-working-parent families just to keep a roof over their heads.

Hard times are just one aspect of this country's growing awareness of the importance of conservation in every facet of our lives. In part, it was the excesses of prior generations which has put us in our present fine mess. But some of the excesses have to do with our own desires for more than we need.

Many of the problems we now face, including the pollution of our air and the contamination of our waters, are the result of rapid industrialization as well as our ignorance about the finite nature of the earth's resources. Like it or not, we have passed the legacy of past and present mistakes onto the next generation. Education has suddenly taken a serious turn, and we must now depend on today's children to solve tomorrow's earth-size problems.

The trick to making your school days fun days is not only to inspire laughter in your classroom so students find learning is something to enjoy. The subject matter must also be *relevant,* and no subject is more relevant than the health of future generations and the planet they will inhabit. Studying the environment in fun ways goes beyond the need to excite young people about the "Three R's." It is perhaps the greatest responsibility and the greatest challenge teachers have ever faced.